THE
WORDS
OF A
PROPHITT

MONTE ALEXANDER

Copyright © 2019 Monte Alexander

All rights reserved. No part of this book may be reproduced, stored, or transmitted by any means—whether auditory, graphic, mechanical, or electronic—without written permission of both publisher and author, except in the case of brief excerpts used in critical articles and reviews. Unauthorized reproduction of any part of this work is illegal and is punishable by law.

*Thank you Susan Murphy
for being my editor and
making me a better author*

CHAPTER ONE

A LONE FIGURE SLOWLY PEDDLED HIS bicycle down the quiet street in the early morning hours on what was promising to be a beautiful day in the Smoky Mountains. The ancient oak trees had grown so large that they had formed a canopy over his route, allowing only a smattering of sunbeams to shine through to the pavement below keeping the temperature cool on a late summer morning. It was the beginning of the fall college term at his alma mater. Since it was the beginning of the school year, most of the students were not yet accustomed to the early classes they were going to have to endure after the summer break or, in the freshmen's case, after graduating from high school. So, the only things stirring were the squirrels playing in the trees and the maintenance men doing their best to keep the campus in pristine condition.

Jacob Prophitt was making his way toward the classroom where he was about to begin his teaching career as a professor at a prestigious Christian university. He had purposely left the house before anyone else was out of bed, so he could be alone with his thoughts, trying to prepare himself mentally for the first day of his new job. Usually he stayed around and helped his wife, Rebecca, get the family up and dressed before he started his day, but because of his state of mind on this day he wanted to avoid the morning disorder that was going to occur. In that house it meant getting five young girls, ranging from age seven to fourteen, ready for their first day of elementary and junior high school. This was a task equal to herding cats, especially doing it with only one and a half bathrooms in the Arts and Crafts bungalow that the University provided as housing for the family on campus. After getting the girls on their way, Rebecca would then have to get their son, who was just starting pre-school, ready for his day as well as getting ready for her job working as a nurse at the local hospital.

    Jacob felt a twinge of guilt as he peddled down the quiet street, hoping that Rebecca would be forgiving. He tried hard to convince himself that she would, knowing that he had been on the verge of making himself sick fretting about the teaching job he had reluctantly accepted from Woodlock University. He had accepted the position because he felt obligated to the University since they helped publish the book he had authored, titled 'The Words of the Prophets'. The book was an outcropping of his doctoral thesis. The journalism department's efforts in promoting the book resulted in it being picked up by a major publishing company. Jacob was paid a generous advance and the book was catching on like wildfire in the theological community. Authoring a book is one thing; however, teaching what he had written was another and he wasn't looking forward to the task.

    Jacob, a tall man standing slightly over six feet and very slender, might be considered by some as too thin. He worked at staying that way by exercising and eating all the right foods. He particularly loved to hike or ride his bike in the surrounding mountains enjoying the tranquility and being close to nature, a passion he had acquired while growing up around his Grampa Eli. His love of the mountains surrounding the community of Woodlock also put a lot of weight on his decision to accept the teaching job there.

Shortly after receiving his Ph.D., Jacob took on the persona of an eclectic man looking the part by sporting a closely-trimmed beard and letting his prematurely salt and pepper hair grow long enough to pull it back into a ponytail. Most of the time he dressed like he was going on a safari, indicative of his love for the outdoors, and wore hiking sandals up to the day it started snowing, and did not change to regular shoes a minute before. He had long forsaken the rock music of his youth and spent his time meditating to the classical music of Bach, Brahms and other renowned classical composers.

Jacob arrived at his destination and peddled up the sidewalk to Peterson Memorial Hall where his classroom was located. While parking his bike in the rack next to the steps at the main entrance, he placed a chain through the spokes on the front rim, thinking to himself, "What a shame I have to padlock this bike, of all places at a Christian university. That's a sad commentary for today's society."

Woodlock Christian University and Seminary was nestled in a valley in the Smoky Mountains in Eastern Tennessee. It was located in the sleepy little town of Woodlock, named after its founding father Jedediah Woodlock. The account of the beginnings of the community was that Jedediah Woodlock settled in the valley after stumbling onto it while on his missionary travels throughout the area a few years after the end of the Revolutionary War. He had traveled from England to the "New World" to convert all of the "heathens", who inhabited the colonies, to the "proper" word of God. He fell in love with the valley when he entered it, taking it as God's call to settle there and teach others to preach the Word, hence the birth of Woodlock Bible Seminary. For the better part of its history the seminary stayed true to its teachings with no exceptions. It began as an all-male school; Jedediah would not allow the temptation of the female allure to distract his future ministers from their calling. The curriculum was strict and based solely on Jedediah's interpretation of the Bible. He was adamant about it being taught in that manner and there was no room for compromise.

Then, as in all things, time moved on and the "old guard" was replaced by the following generations and their new ideas; the landscape of Jedediah's dream was altered. The school had to survive financially and was unable to do that resting on its past history. Eventually the school became co-ed and its curriculum was altered to meet the modern times. The focus changed from being strictly a Bible seminary, teaching the philosophies of Jedediah Woodlock, to a college teaching a diverse program of studies including accounting, business, financing, and management. Because of those changes the teaching staffs now included a Rabbi, an Imam and, yes, even a Catholic Priest, which a hard-driving, pulpit-pounding Protestant like Jedediah Woodlock would have never allowed. Woodlock University and Bible Seminary had evolved into a school that produced more church administrators than preachers and its graduates were highly sought out by any church looking to grow, especially the mega-churches that were desirous of packed sanctuaries and full collection plates.

Many felt that poor ole' Jedediah was still turning over in his grave because of the changes. There were a few who claimed that they had seen and heard Jedediah's spirit walking the halls of Peterson Hall, one of the oldest buildings on campus, moaning and shaking his head in disgust.

Jacob removed his helmet and looked up at the ivied walls and tall glass entrance of the more than a century old building and let out a huge sigh. The thought of teaching about a subject from the Bible, the book that was causing him to question his faith, to a bunch of young adults who mostly had to be there for the required credit hours, was not appealing to him at that very moment. Under his breath he asked, "What the heck am I doing here?" He continued standing there considering unlocking his bike and riding away. Jacob then let out another long sigh and reluctantly walked toward the building and then bounded up the half-dozen steps to the entrance, entering the heavy wood and leaded glass doors. From the landing inside the doors he had another flight of stairs to climb to reach the main floor of the hall where his classroom was located. With his thoughts still somewhere out in the universe, when he was halfway up the flight of stairs, he was startled by a loud greeting from an unnoticed figure standing above him at the top of the stairs.

"GOOD MORNIN' DOCTOR PROPHITT! HOW Y'ALL DOIN' ON THIS BEAUTIFUL MORNIN'? I'VE BEEN LOOKIN' FORWARD TO MAKIN' YER ACQUAINTANCE!"

A startled Jacob stopped on the steps and looked up to see a short, fairly young, slightly overweight man with a beard and closely cropped black hair, wearing a yellow Polo shirt, khaki slacks, tasseled loafers and wearing a kippah. Jacob thought to himself, "Wow, a little too preppy for my taste."

Before Jacob could respond, the preppy figure continued in his heavy southern accent, "Hi, I'm Rabbi Aaron Weiss, yer one-man welcomin' committee and a big fan of yer work. Please call me Aaron."

Jacob paused on the steps gathering his thoughts as he was not only startled by the loud greeting, but also stunned that this was a Rabbi at a Christian school. Still recovering from the shock given by his greeter, he composed himself while beginning to pull the straps of the backpack off of his shoulders and responded. "Well, Aaron . . . I thank you for the warm welcome. I must admit I did not expect a greeting committee, let alone the one person in the world that is a fan of my book." Jacob completed his climb up the stairway and held out his hand to his greeter.

Rabbi Weiss was having a hearty laugh at Jacob's comment while he grabbed Jacob's hand and gave him an over-enthusiastic handshake. "Ohhhhhh contraire Dr. Prophitt; I believe there's a lot more people in the business of teachin' the word of God that are greatly impressed with yer book than just me. That's a true piece of inspiration. Come, join me in the lounge; I have a pot of coffee brewin'. Y'all drink coffee don't ya?"

Jacob, still a bit unsettled by this preppy, good ole' boy whirlwind, was thinking that this guy had already had too much coffee by this time of the morning. He followed his new acquaintance down the hallway and through a door into the professors' lounge. The whole time Rabbi Weiss was talking at cyber speed and Jacob was not hearing a word he said until he was shaken back to reality by, "Doctor Prophitt! How do ya take yer coffee?"

"Uh . . . black with sweetener, no sugar."

"Doughnut?"

"No, never touch the stuff, but one of those bananas looks pretty good."

Laughing, the Rabbi responded, "I think y'all can tell that pastries are an important part of my diet. Is there anything else I can get ya?"

"No, coffee and a banana are fine."

"Sure Doc! Oh, I'm sorry I forgot my manners. How would ya prefer to be addressed . . . Doc, Doctor Prophitt, or Professor Prophitt? Y'all tell me."

THE WORDS OF A PROPHITT

Jacob had to mull this over for a moment as he had not considered how he would like to be addressed by colleagues or students in this unfamiliar environment, something totally foreign to him. "I guess since you insist on being addressed as Aaron, we should dispense of the formalities and you can just call me Jacob."

Rabbi Weiss stopped working at the coffee pot for a moment and turned his attention toward his colleague, "Ahhhh, Jacob. That's a name near and dear to my heart as ya can well imagine. Okay, Jacob it is. I usually have a tough time rememberin' first names, but yer's won't be a problem." He turned back to the job at hand and continued, "If there's one name synonymous with my heritage, it's Jacob. I wouldn't dare ever forget that name. But why am I tellin' y'all? You're a Bible scholar with a doctorate and have probably forgotten more than I'll ever know 'bout the important names of the Hebrew Bible. I sometimes think . . ."

Jacob suddenly started laughing out loud and Rabbi Weiss stopped what he was saying and turned back to Jacob with a confused look. "Aaron, have you inhaled a breath of air since I got here?"

The Rabbi stayed quiet for a moment and then a sheepish grin came over his face and he inhaled a deep breath. "I've been talkin' too much haven't I? I've gotta apologize; I tend to do that when I'm nervous."

Jacob stood up to accept the cup of coffee and the fruit being handed to him by his host, "What in the world do you have to be nervous about? This is my first day of teaching; I'm the rookie here, and I assume you're an experienced professor. I'm the nervous one; I have no idea what I'm even doing here or even how to go about teaching these classes."

Rabbi Weiss, now more subdued and paying attention to Jacob, took a sip of coffee as he moved over to the table in the middle of the room, sat down and leaned back in his chair. After a long pause, as if in deep thought, he spoke. "Yeah Jacob, I've been doin' this for a while, and let me tell you somethin', this teachin' thing's not hard to do. Y'all have a wealth of knowledge to give and yer gonna have a lecture room full of young sponges wantin' to learn what ya know. I assume ya have a teachin' plan in place don't ya?"

"Sure, I do; I've been working on it all summer. I just hope I didn't miss anything, I don't want to look like an uneducated idiot to a bunch of kids trying to get a decent education."

With a look of disbelief, the Rabbi gazed at his new acquaintance and blurted out, "Uneducated idiot! Whatcha talkin' 'bout? Y'all are the author of a book that's settin' the theologians on their ears! Y'all have gained a lot of esteem among the staff and alumni here, and these students know that. How in the world do ya think yer gonna look like an idiot to them? Wake up and smell the coffee Jacob. Yer in the driver's seat. Trust me, those kids will wanna hear yer words. The only thing ya need to be concerned with is the fact that the words ya speak could have a profound impact on the future of these people plannin' on workin' in the business of spreadin' the word of God."

Jacob leaned forward in his chair, placing his elbows on the table, peering into his coffee cup not looking up at his colleague sitting across from him, pondering the words that had just been spoken. Unfortunately for Jacob, they weren't words of comfort; actually, they added additional anxiety, something he didn't need at this time of the morning, especially on this day. After a few moments of silence, Jacob took a deep breath and let out a huge sigh and finally responded, "Aaron, I can't believe that I am sharing this with you, but I'm not sure I can go into that hall with a good conscience and teach this subject. I'm struggling with my faith. If I'm not sure about my belief in God, how can I teach the word of God?" He then paused and looked up and gave a nervous chuckle and asked, "Why in the world am I telling all this to a Rabbi who sounds like a good ole boy from the deep South?"

A solemn smile came across Aaron's face as he looked at the conflicted person on the other side of the table. Taking his time before saying anything, he wanted to be sure on how to respond to what Jacob had just uttered without upsetting him. "We Rabbis have that effect on people Jacob." After a little chuckle at his attempt at humor he continued, "As far as my accent, I grew up in Atlanta, Georgia so I come by it honest. There are Jews in the South ya know. Contrary to popular belief, not all of us come from New York City, and as far as talkin' 'bout your faith issue, I like to think my most important job is to be an ear to those that have a problem. Let me ask ya this, why are y'all havin' an issue with yer faith?"

Jacob felt some heat coming down from the top of his head, not ready to fully open up with a person he had just met about his deepest innermost feelings. Reluctantly he responded, "It's complicated; I don't think there is any one thing that is causing my non-belief."

"Non-belief? Jacob, a second ago y'all said ya weren't sure about yer belief, and now ya use the word non-belief. Which is it?

Jacob could feel the heat in his face welling up even more as he fired back, "Aaron, you're getting awful technical, aren't you?! Maybe we shouldn't continue this conversation!"

"Sorry, sorry, just askin' questions. That's just the counselor trainin' comin' outta me. I didn't mean anything by it. Heck, questionin' yer faith isn't anything new around here. I would guess that most of the teachin' staff at this school has questioned their faith at some time or another. I know I have."

Jacob felt the heat in his face subside somewhat as Aaron backed off. He got up from the table and walked over to the coffee maker to refill his cup. As he returned to the table, Aaron continued the questioning.

"Tell me about your book Jacob. It's truly a great accomplishment; I can't believe some of the insights that have come to me from it. How did ya ever find the words to write such a thing?"

Jacob felt a twinge of embarrassment since he had not been comfortable with all of this celebrity stuff. Taking a sip of his coffee, he acted as if he was giving careful consideration to the answer he was about to provide to his interrogator. "I'm not sure; I think it just came from necessity. I had gotten my Master's Degree and decided to go for my doctorate and needed a subject when I had to write my thesis. Both my father and grandfather were involved in the ministry and I grew up with the Bible, and one of the parts of the Bible that always fascinated me was the prophets. To most people they are boring, but for some reason that wasn't the case for me, so I decided to write about that subject and began to study it in depth, then one thing led to another. As I was compiling the information it seemed like I would go down one path and it would lead to another and the information would corroborate; then I would go down another path, and then another. Somehow it all came together in a neat package. I would go to bed with questions and literally wake up in the middle of the night with ways to find the answers. It was kind of weird, but it worked. That's it in a nutshell."

The Rabbi got up from his chair and returned to the box of pastry, reaching for his second helping while continuing the conversation, "I guess ya could say that God put those facts in yer head so ya could share them with the world."

"Yeah, I guess you could say that. You could also say that the whole thing is nothing but dumb luck!"

Aaron, again feeling the edginess in Jacobs's words, decided to change the subject. "My wife Mindy saw a family movin' in down the street from us the other day in the bungalow the university owns. Was that y'all?"

Jacob, glad for the change of subject again felt a little more comfortable with his interrogator. "Yeah, it was probably us. We moved from an overcrowded apartment to an overcrowded house. I still consider it a move up though."

"Mindy says y'all have a big family. How many kids ya got?"

"We have six, five girls ranging from seven to fourteen years and a five-year-old son."

Aaron started laughing and exclaimed, "Wow, I bet ya don't have enough bathrooms in that little house to take care of all those girls, especially the older ones gettin' in their teens."

"Yeah, it's proving to be a challenge some days, and I'm sure this morning was like a zoo for my wife, with me leaving early." Again, Jacob felt a little twinge of guilt for leaving Rebecca alone with the task.

"Okay, Jacob, here's the test . . . can ya remember all their names at this time of the mornin'?"

"Sure, I can, they're my flesh and blood. How could I possibly forget their names? Bethany is the oldest, then Ruth, Mary, Martha, and Esther. We named our son Ezekiel. Ezekiel Eli Prophitt; we call him Zeke for short. His middle name comes from my Grandpa Eli."

Aaron noticed Jacob's eyes light up when he started talking about his son, even more so than when he was nam-ing his daughters. He wasn't sure why, but he began to sense an issue within the Prophitt family, and maybe a reason for Jacob's uncertainty about his faith. Aaron took a big bite out of a jelly roll and immediately washed it down with a swig of coffee. "Jacob Prophitt, y'all are unbelievable. Ya have achieved gettin' a PH. D, written a book that'll probably be on a best seller list, landed a teachin' job at a prestigious Christian university, and on top of that ya have five girls and a son, and probably a beautiful wife that has born all of these children and has been there to support ya through all that. Most people in the world would only hope of doin' one of the things you have accomplished. Ya have been truly blessed by the hand of God Himself. What's really goin' on with y'all; how in the world could ya not believe? My friend, I sense that there's more to what is goin' on inside ya than just a lack of faith in God."

There they were . . . the words Jacob didn't want to hear, the same words he had been hearing from just about everyone around him for months. Jacob suddenly felt the heat permeate through his entire body, and his face felt like it was in flames. He tried to keep his composure in responding, but his anger suddenly overtook his faculties and he responded in a terse manner to the question, "I will tell you why I don't believe in God. My son, the future of my family lineage, has been given an early death sentence. My wife and I were trying to have a son and we had five girls before he was born, and then when he finally arrived, in a few short months into his life, he was diagnosed with an incurable disease that more than likely will prevent him from reaching his twenties. I have a tough time believing that a loving God would allow that to happen to an innocent little boy. Rabbi, you may think I have been blessed by the hand of God, but I can't buy into that. If anything, I have been cursed. If there is a God, and he has a hand in anything I have accomplished, then the end result of all those accomplishments is a cruel joke on me."

Aaron leaned back in his chair with a solemn look, knowing that he had struck emotional oil, hitting the nerve that was causing his new colleague to question his faith. He again took a long pause to contemplate his next move, not wanting to enrage Jacob further but rather to find the words that would bring calmness back to the conversation. The air in the room had become very thick with tension and Aaron knew from years of counseling others that the significance of saying the right words at this very moment was extremely important. He did not want to antagonize Jacob, possibly causing him to pull away ruining any chance of helping him find a way to deal with his personal conflict.

Aaron noticed that the fire in Jacob's eyes had been subsiding ever so slightly and decided it was safe to move ahead. Slowly moving his pastry plate and coffee cup aside, Aaron leaned forward clasping his hands before him on the table, still being deliberate before saying any words. Finally, with a solemn look on his face, he asked, "Jacob, what's wrong with Ezekiel?

Jacobs's eyes teared up slightly and he took a deep breath, "He was diagnosed with Cystic Fibrosis."

Aaron sat back in his chair feeling like he had just been stabbed in the chest. The thought of a young child being burdened with such an affliction was heartbreaking to him. "Wow, Jacob, that's a tough one. I'm so sorry. I know y'all feel pain over the situation with yer son, and I also know it's painful for ya to hear other people say yer blessed; however, ya need to understand that yer not the only person in the world to face adversity along with the blessin's God has given them. As I said before, questionin' yer faith is not unique to just you. Heck, there was a time when I seriously considered givin' up on this Rabbi business."

Jacob was surprised hearing these words. He had to let things sink in for a moment before he could respond. "You thought about not being a Rabbi? What happened for you to consider that?"

Aaron again leaned forward in his chair, again clasping his hands in front of him, hoping he could keep his composure while giving an explanation, as the subject was still something that was heavy on his heart. Finally, he mustered up enough courage to begin. "Mindy and I met in college and immediately fell in love; it was love at first sight. All we could talk about when we were datin' was how many little ones we'd have after we got married since we both have soooo much love in us for children. After we got hitched, we tried to start a family and nothin' was happenin'. After several visits to fertility doctors it was determined that we couldn't have any babies. It just wasn't meant to be so I started questionin' my faith. Why would God allow that to happen to two people that wanted children as much as Mindy and I did? I got real down on myself and decided to do somethin' else. I didn't feel I could in good faith continue doin' the work of a God that allowed bad things to happen."

"So, what changed your mind? You are obviously still a Rabbi."

"Well, I decided to take a step back and pray for guidance rather than make a rash decision. I took some time off and did some volunteer work at a community center in Atlanta that our Synagogue sponsored. It gave kids who live in tough neighborhoods a place to go to avoid the bad that sometimes can suck them in and ruin their lives. While workin' there it occurred to me that there's a lotta kids out there that are hurtin'. Some kids live in a one-parent home, or maybe even a home with no parents; just grandparents or aunts or uncles. I also found out that most of those kids were eager to learn if someone was willin' to spend time with them and teach them somethin'. I would see their eyes light up when they found out somethin' new, and it made me feel good. Mindy was already teachin' in grade school; she loved her job and shared with me that she felt the same way I did when she saw a light go on with a kid. So, I decided that God wanted me to teach; I also decided that the best way I could do that was to teach what I know best, the Word of God. I let go of the dream of havin' children and focused on makin' the lives of our younger generation better through education. I have this theory that God sometimes allows us to experience a lack of faith in order to open our eyes to other possibilities."

Jacob again felt a strong twinge of guilt; however, this time it had nothing to do with his slipping out early to avoid the early morning chaos at home. This feeling of guilt came from him and Rebecca having a large family compared to Aaron and Mindy not being able to have any children at all. All of the irritation he had felt earlier from Aaron's questioning had subsided; he was ashamed that he was not feeling blessed, but at the same time he was still mad at God because of his son's illness.

Aaron watched the expression on the face of the man sitting across the table from him. Jacob had been looking right at him, but more like looking through him. It was almost like "the lights were on but nobody was home" and Aaron could sense that he had hit a nerve or two. Making the decision to break the staring contest with his table mate, he got up from the table to retrieve another unneeded cup of coffee. While standing at the counter pouring his coffee, Aaron heard Jacob begin to speak.

"Aaron, I am so sorry."

Rabbi Weiss turned around and saw Jacob sitting with his elbows on the table and his face cradled in his hands. The Rabbi quietly walked back to his seat at the table giving his troubled associate time to collect his thoughts. After a moment he responded, "Jacob, ya don't need to feel sorry. We're doin' okay; we've come to grips with our fate and doin' quite well in spite of it. Ya'll need to do the same."

Again, the room was quiet. Jacob had not moved a muscle and Aaron wasn't sure if his colleague was weeping or just pondering the words he had just spoken. He allowed the silence to permeate the room for a few more minutes and then decided to move in with some questions that were burning in his heart to ask. "Jacob, I know that we've just met, and we've shared a lot in the last hour or so and I feel comfortable and compelled to ask you something. Answering this question honestly to yerself might help give y'all a new perspective on this issue with yer faith."

Jacob sat motionless for a few more moments and then slowly lowered his hands from his face looking up at Aaron. His eyes were still clear and, much to Aaron's relief, showed that he had not been crying, but just sitting in silence. Nervously clearing his throat before speaking, Jacob finally spoke, "What is the question Rabbi?"

"Jacob, I don't wanna offend ya by askin'. We don't have to do this if ya don't wanna."

"It's okay, go ahead. I'm a grown man . . . I can take it."

"Are ya sure? I don't want ya goin' all freaky on me and start swingin' at me."

Jacob smiled and sat back in his chair, appreciating his interrogator's attempt at easing the tension in the room, "No Aaron, I'm not going to start swinging at you. I'm basically a peaceful sort of person. Go ahead and ask. We've already reached into some pretty deep personal conversation already between new acquaintances. What difference is another hard question going to make?"

"Okay, here goes. Would ya be as upset about this situation if one of yer daughters was diagnosed with the disease rather than yer son?"

Jacob's eyes were suddenly on fire and he sat forward in his chair as if he was going to climb over the table toward his interviewer. "Aaron, that is absurd! How could you even ask such a thing! That is . . . uh that is . . . I mean that question is . . . how can you even . . ." Then Jacob suddenly went quiet and the fire went out of his eyes. He slumped back into his chair with a dumfounded expression on his face staring at Aaron. After sitting quietly for a moment deep in thought, he finally replied, "I don't know why, but that is a very tough question. I don't think I can give you an honest answer right now."

Aaron arose from the table gathering his plate and cup. He carried them to the sink, rinsed them off and placed them in the dishwasher. When he was done with his chore, he turned back to see Jacob still sitting in silence with the same expression on his face. He walked over to him, placed a hand on his shoulder for a moment and then headed for the door, "Jacob y'all don't have to give me an answer. Ya need to find the answer fer yerself. Shalom, my friend."

Jacob turned in his chair, watching Aaron head for the door. "Is it time for your class Aaron?"

Aaron, just about to pull the door open and leave, stopped. "Nope, I don't have any classes today."

"Then why were you here this morning?"

Aaron turned facing Jacob with a broad smile. "I'm not really sure. I just felt compelled to be here to meet y'all. Funny how that happens, isn't it? Now I think I'll go down to the coffee shop and try to convert some young Christians over to my side."

Jacob suddenly had a look of disbelief on his face because of what Aaron had just said; he blurted out, "*Really?*"

Aaron started laughing. "No, not really, that's just a little rabbinic humor. But I have to admit the look on yer face was priceless. See ya later Doctor Prophitt." Aaron exited leaving Jacob alone with his thoughts.

Jacob's mind was going at cyber speed, trying to make sense of the conversation he had just had with the Rabbi. He looked up at the clock on the wall across from where he was sitting and decided that he had better head for his classroom to get ready for his first session as a professor. He got up from his chair and gathered his utensils, took them to the counter sink, rinsed them off and placed them in the dishwasher just as Aaron had done. He went back to the table, picked up his backpack and walked to the door preparing to exit. He placed his hand on the door handle, paused and took a deep breath before pulling it open, saying under his breath, "Okay, I can do this."

CHAPTER TWO

JACOB PULLED OPEN THE DOOR and entered the room where he was about to begin the next chapter in his life. He was immediately met with the smell of new paint that had been applied during the summer to spruce up the old building. The classroom was designed as a lecture hall, with eight tiers slightly arched around the main floor where the teacher's podium and desk were located. Behind the desk the wall was covered halfway up with a blackboard. The floors were made from wide wooden planks that had been polished to a high shine and probably had a century of layers of varnish on them. The tiers were lined with old wooden classroom desks that looked very uncomfortable and had probably been there since the building was erected. Jacob, still thinking about his conversation with Rabbi Weiss, laid his backpack on the desk and started pulling out his paperwork in preparation for the students who would soon be shuffling into the room. As he was sitting down at the desk preparing to take one last scan of his teaching notes, he was startled by the sound of snoring. Looking up to the top corner of the room he noticed a lone figure sitting with his head lying on the desktop. Speaking in a voice loud enough to get the attention of his sleeping inhabitant Jacob commented, "Good morning, you're here early."

The sleeping figure stirred lifting up his head, barely awake, replied, "yeah . . . uh . . . good mornin' to you too." Then he moved around in his seat and lay his head back against the wall behind him attempting to go back to sleep.

"Looks like you are having a tough time waking up."

The individual raised his head again with his eyes opening a little wider, "uh . . . yeah I . . . uh, I drove all night to get here. Sorry, I'll be okay in a minute." Then he lay his head back against the wall, starting to snore again.

Jacob wondered to himself why anyone would have to drive all night to make it to class, and then started taking more notice of the person sitting asleep at the desk. He appeared to be a man in his early fifties with thick black hair which was gray around the edges, combed straight back being held in place with some type of grease, and a lot of it. The guy needed a shave and was dressed like he had just walked off a golf course, wearing dark gray slacks and a black sweater vest over a white short-sleeve Polo shirt. Then, shaking his head in disbelief, Jacob noticed that the guy was wearing black and white saddle oxford shoes with golf spikes.

Sitting down at his desk, Jacob continued to stare at the lone figure sleeping at the far corner of the room contemplating what had occurred during his day so far. He was hoping that, at some point, he would reach some semblance of what could be considered normal. However, looking up at the guy asleep in the corner of the room, he wasn't too sure it was going to occur during the class session that was about to begin.

Suddenly, Jacob was returned to reality when the classroom door swung open and four normal-acting young students entered, talking and laughing while making their way up the steps and locating desks to sit at. Letting out a sigh of relief, Jacob got up, picked up a piece of chalk and began writing information on the blackboard as more students filtered into the room. Even with all the noise of shuffling desks and conversations going on, he could still hear an occasional snore from the man sitting at the desk at the top corner of the room. After finishing his chalk work on the board, Jacob returned to his desk, waiting just a few more minutes before starting class, to make sure that all of the students were settled in.

When Jacob decided it was safe to begin, he got up and took his place behind the podium, cleared his throat and began by saying . . . "Good morning ladies and gentlemen, welcome to my class. We, as a group, are going to embark on an in-depth study of the prophets of the Old Testament. My name is Doctor Jacob Prophitt and I will be your professor. I prefer to be addressed as Doctor Prophitt during our time together here in the classroom. When you registered for this class you were given instructions on what text will be used. It is titled 'The Words of the Prophets' of which I am the author. Also, upon registration you should have been given instructions to read the first chapter in preparation for our class today. I hope most of you at least opened the book and looked at the index."

At that point several laughs and snickers came from the students, the result Jacob hoped for, trying to add a little levity to the session. Then another loud snore came from the top corner of the room. Jacob looked up and noticed that his early arrival was opening his eyes, moving around, and then once again lay his head back against the wall and going back to sleep. The rest of the students found that amusing and again broke out in laughter.

Jacob picked up a piece of paper from the corner of his desk, walked over to one of the students at the front of the class, handed it to him and then instructed all of the class,

"I am going to pass this around and I would like for you to write your name down so I can make note of your attendance. Please give it to the person next to you until it passes all the way around the room." Then raising his voice to a much louder volume he remarked, "AND WHEN WE GATHER FOR OUR NEXT SESSION, I WOULD HOPE THAT EVERYONE WILL HAVE HAD ENOUGH SLEEP SO THAT THEY CAN STAY AWAKE DURING CLASS!"

The man in the corner again snorted, moved a little, opened his eyes for a moment, raised his hand in acknowledgement to the instructor, and then lay his head back closing his eyes again. Jacob then decided it was useless and made a mental note to himself to have this person taken before the Dean of Students.

Gathering his composure, he continued, "During this class term we will be probing into the purpose of the prophets and discussing in great detail all of the prophets, both major and minor, all the way from Moses to Malachi. We will be paying particular attention to the prophecies indicating the anticipated coming of a Messiah. You will find in my book that I have not only used the Bible as a reference about these prophets, but also that I have included information from the rabbinic legends that I was able to find through extensive research."

Jacob paused for a few moments to consider his next words and to let what he had just said sink in with his students, at least to the ones who were paying attention. Then he continued; "Now it's obvious we will have a lot of material to cover during this term, so I want to set some ground rules so we don't get bogged down in unimportant details. We are here to learn about the prophets and only the prophets. I do not care to get into discussions about theology or faith in God. I feel those are personal issues and I am sure you will be covering those subjects in other theology classes, so let's leave it at that. I will be lecturing, and I will allow questions during my lectures as long as they are directly related to the subject. Is that fair enough for all of you?"

Knowing that it was a rhetorical question since he was the one making the rules, he was pleased with himself as he looked around the room and saw eager and smiling faces shaking their heads in agreement. Then another snore came from the corner of the room, adding to the irritation Jacob was feeling related to his sleeping attendee. Again, he decided to try to ignore the interruption and go on with his lecture. "Okay, let's get started. I am going to begin by diagramming the timelines of the prophets and when they were active during the Israelite history in the Old Testament, so you can better understand what was taking place with the Hebrews during those time periods. Doing that makes it easier to make sense of what they were prophesying about."

Jacob left his podium, picked up a piece of chalk and began drawing on the blackboard and lecturing. During the session the students appeared to be intent on what he was saying. Occasionally one of the students would raise a question, but things went rather smoothly for the new teacher in his first day of class, other than dealing with "Sleeping Beauty".

Time flew by for Jacob and he couldn't believe that his class time was almost over when he glanced at his watch. So, he began to wind down his lecture. He completed the last part of his diagram, put down the chalk and returned to his podium for some finishing words, "This diagram should provide you with a roadmap about our subject matter as we go through this term. In our next session we will discuss, in length, Moses. I recommend that you read the next two chapters of our text and outline the information, so you will be prepared. Everyone, have a good day, and whoever has the attendance sheet please bring it to my desk. Thank you."

At once all the students started moving around, packing their computers and lesson material in bags and backpacks, talking and laughing as they started shuffling out of the room. Some of them offered thanks and pleasantries to the Professor as they passed by his desk. Jacob looked up in the corner of the room to see his sleeping gnome awake and writing on a notepad. The guy closed the pad and put it in his shirt pocket under his sweater. He then got up, sidestepped down the row of seats to the steps, and then began descending from the top tier of the room, taking slow deliberate steps down to the main floor. Now that the man was not sitting at a desk, Jacob could see that the guy was a couple of inches short of being six feet tall and that he was stocky, not fat except for a little extra belly, but for the most part in good physical condition. With a huge grin on his face as he approached Jacob, he said, "Man, it's tough walkin' on these polished hardwood floors with golf spikes."

Jacob looked up as the last student left the room, and with a perturbed expression replied, with a tone of sarcasm in his voice, "Yes I am certain it is difficult walking on these floors with those golf shoes. May I suggest more appropriate attire for your feet when attending the next session Mister . . . ?"

"Uh . . . yeah, my name is Michael, Michael D'Angelo."

Jacob took the attendance sheet from his hand, perused it and remarked, "Mister D'Angelo it seems that you haven't signed in for class. Is there a problem? You certainly didn't appear to be very interested in what I had to say today."

"Uh . . . oh no Doc, I'm not a student, I'm here to observe. Here, let me give you my card." He then reached into his back pocket, pulling out a well-worn wallet, and began digging through a thick mess of what looked like receipts protruding from it and finally, located a card which he handed to Jacob. Taking a long, hard look at his visitor before inspecting the information on the somewhat faded and crumpled card, Jacob peered at it and read "Michael D'Angelo, Recruiter, Cosmos Industries Unlimited".

"So . . . Mister D'Angelo . . ."

"Please, call me Michael."

"So . . . Mister D'Angelo, what is your business here? I certainly did not appreciate the interruption to my class session with your snoring."

"Sorry about that Doc . . ."

"It's Doctor Prophitt!"

"Oh . . . yeah . . . sorry about that Doc, I got a late start leavin' the golf course down in Augusta and had to drive all night to get here, so I'm a little tired. I didn't even get a chance to stop by my locker and get my street shoes when I realized I was running so late. We got a little tied up at the nineteenth hole . . . if you know what I mean."

Jacob rolled his eyes at the lack of manners he was experiencing from his visitor and continued his questioning, "I know what you mean, but why are you here?"

"Like I said, I'm here to observe your work."

"Mister D'Angelo, I'm not sure that you have the authority to sit in on my classes. There must be some protocol the University has about such things."

"Oh, sure Doc, it's all legal. I have a letter right here from President Upton, giving me permission to sit in on your sessions. Here, let me show you." He then started feeling around and digging into all his pockets not finding it. Then he suddenly said, "Oh, here it is, right here in my back pocket. Right where I thought it was."

Jacob took the mutilated envelope from his visitor and removed a letter trying to smooth it out, so he could read it. After scanning the letter, he looked up at D'Angelo, "It looks legitimate, but I still don't know why you would be observing what I am doing in my class."

"My Boss sent me to observe you in the classroom and to meet you to see if you would be a suitable candidate to work with His organization. He read that little book of yours and was very impressed, so he sent me to check you out."

"That's all fine Mister D'Angelo . . ."

"Michael . . . please call me Michael."

"I prefer to stick with being formal if you don't mind."

"Okay Doc, suit yourself."

Letting out a long, disgusted sigh, Jacob then continued, "Anyway, Mister D'Angelo, I just started this job and I have no intention of leaving here anytime soon, so I believe you have wasted a trip on my account."

"Oh, no prob Doc, I have to go where my Boss sends me; it ain't any skin off my nose. I will tell you that if my Boss likes you and wants you, it won't interfere with your present job. In fact, it will work quite well with what you're doin'."

"Well, Mister D'Angelo, I would doubt that your employer would be very happy to hear that you spent your time sleeping when you were supposed to be observing my work."

"Yeah, about that Doc, I was multitasking."

"Are you serious? Mister D'Angelo you were snoring the whole time. You want me to believe you were paying attention to what I was saying?"

"Yeah Doc, I'll prove it to ya. You started out by sayin', *"Good morning ladies and gentlemen, welcome to my class where we are going to embark on an in-depth study of the prophets of the Old Testament. My name is Doctor Jacob Prophitt and I will be your instructor. I prefer to be addressed as Doctor Prophitt during our time together here in the classroom. When you registered for this class you were given instructions on what text will be used. It is titled 'The Words of the Prophets' of which I am the author. Also, upon registration you should have been given instructions to read the first chapter in preparation for our class today. I hope most of you at least opened the book and looked at the index.* Then there was a tee hee, ha ha, giggle giggle. Then you went on to say, *I am going to pass this paper around and I would like for you to write your name down, so I can make note of your attendance. Please pass it on to the person next to you until it passes all the way around the room.* Then you raised your voice and said, AND WHEN WE GATHER FOR OUR NEXT SESSION, I WOULD HOPE THAT EVERYONE WILL HAVE HAD ENOUGH SLEEP SO THAT THEY CAN STAY AWAKE DURING CLASS!"

"Okay, I guess you were . . ."

"And then you went on to talk about how you didn't want discussions about theology or faith and how you wanted to stick to the subject . . ."

"OKAY . . . okay Mister D'Angelo, I've heard enough. I don't know how you did it, but apparently you *were* listening to what I was saying."

"Just like I said Doc, multi-tasking."

Jacob took a long hard look at the man standing in front of his desk, then peered back down at the business card laying in front of him and wished the guy would just go away so he could pack up his class materials and go. Then thinking better of it, commented, "So, Mister D'Angelo, tell me more about this Cosmos Industries Unlimited that you represent."

"You know what Professor?" Jacob felt another twinge of frustration shoot down his spine. "I'd love to do just that, but I'm starvin' after drivin' all night and not havin' any breakfast. Let me make it up to ya and buy ya lunch. I saw an interesting lookin' greasy spoon a couple of blocks down the street that caught my eye when I was drivin' through the campus. I love to eat in those places. They usually have great food. Pack up your stuff and I'll drive us down there and we can continue this discussion while we eat."

Jacob considered this to be an opportunity to blow this guy off and get out of an unpleasant situation. "I tell you what Mister D'Angelo; you go ahead to the diner and have lunch. I'll pack up my 'stuff' as you call it, and I may or may not join you. I'll decide in a few minutes."

"Okay, suit yourself Doc, but you should at least learn a little more about the organization. I think you'll like what I have to say. Tell you what . . . I'll see you there." Turning away and walking gingerly on his golf spikes toward the door, he stopped and turned back to Jacob, "It would be a good idea to give me a little time to get out to the car since these floors are so slick."

Jacob watched him exit through the door, leaned back in his chair looking up at the ceiling as if he was looking at the heavens, let out a huge sigh of relief, wondering to himself what he had done to deserve these interruptions he had experienced, especially on the first day at his new job.

After a few moments of silence, Jacob decided it was safe to leave the classroom. Getting out of his chair, he began shoving his computer and teaching material into his backpack and headed for the exit. Opening the door, he looked both ways in the hallway to see if anyone was there. Not seeing any movement anywhere, he decided it was safe to venture out and leave Peterson Hall. Rushing down the steps to the leaded glass doors, he pushed one side open and slowly exited, looking around to see if there was anybody he wanted to avoid lurking around. When he decided it was safe to continue, he climbed down the last flight of steps and walked over to his bike. While unlocking it he again looked around to see if anyone was waiting anywhere around. He straddled the seat, climbed on, pushed off, and headed out into the street pedaling in the opposite direction of the diner heading for home. After riding along for a couple of blocks, for some unknown reason, he made a U-turn and started peddling toward the diner, the entire time muttering under his breath, "I'm going to regret this, I just know it."

CHAPTER THREE

J ACOB ARRIVED AT THE DINER and immediately noticed a long, shiny black Mercedes Benz parked at the curb. Noting that it had Georgia license plates and not being the kind of car, you would see around Woodlock, he assumed it belonged to D'Angelo. Dismounting and locking his bike to a parking meter, he stopped and took another deep breath, still trying to decide if he was going to go through with having lunch with this guy or better yet go home. After another moment or two, he relented and headed for the entrance. Opening the door and walking into the packed diner, he was immediately startled by a loud voice yelling over the noise of conversation and the rattling of dishes and silverware, "HEY DOC, OVER HERE!" Jacob looked over in a corner of the diner to see D'Angelo seated at a table with a waitress standing next to him. Lowering his face in hopes of not being noticed by the rest of the lunch crowd, he wormed his way through the throng of tables toward his seat. When he arrived at the table he looked down and noticed that D'Angelo was now wearing a pair of fuzzy bunny slippers with floppy ears that were long enough to hang over the toes of them. Closing his eyes and shaking his head in disgust, Jacob considered turning around and running out of the diner, but then reluctantly peeled off his backpack, laying it on the floor and took his seat.

"What do ya think Doc? Nice lookin' slippers, ain't they? I found these in the trunk of the car. I had forgotten that I had them. They're a heck of a lot easier to walk around in than golf shoes with spikes."

Jacob, now wishing he had gone straight home, and still considering getting up and leaving, replied in a sarcastic tone, "Uh, yeah, nice touch Mister D'Angelo. They certainly add an air of professionalism to your ensemble."

Letting out a hearty laugh, D'Angelo responded, "You are a funny guy Doc. Say hello to our waitress, Marci. I've been chatting with her and it ends up she is one of your students."

Jacob looked up at the smiling face of the young lady who was holding a notepad, awaiting the order from her customers. Jacob smiled back at her, "Good afternoon Marci. I do remember seeing you in class this morning. I hope it was a pleasant experience for you."

Marci's smile grew even broader after hearing that he recognized her and she could barely hold back her enthusiasm, "Gee Doctor Prophitt, I really enjoyed your lecture this morning. I learned a lot. I probably shouldn't have done this, but I enjoyed your book so much that I have already read the whole thing. I hope that isn't a problem."

"Oh no, Marci, that will not be a problem. I am flattered that you liked the book enough to have read it entirely already. I am sure it will give you a head start on the rest of the class."

"Doctor Prophitt, I'm not the only one. I know of several people in the class that couldn't put it down once they started reading it." Jacob felt humbled by her statement, wondering why there would be such an interest, especially from a group of young adults on a subject he had chosen to write about, which would be considered by most to be as interesting as watching paint dry. Marci then brought the subject back to food, "Okay gentlemen, what would you like to have for lunch?"

Jacob picked up the lunch menu in front of him, gave it a quick look-over, not seeing anything that would be appropriate for his Spartan diet. Looking up at Marci he inquired, "Can I get a side salad with Italian dressing and a glass of water with a lemon?"

"Sure, Doctor Prophitt, not a problem." Looking over at D'Angelo, she asked, "How about you sir?"

"Marci, I want that two-third pound country bacon burger with extra bacon and a double order of cheese fries and a large Pepsi."

"Sorry sir, we have Coke products, no Pepsi."

Suddenly D'Angelo broke out in a boisterous laugh that could be heard throughout the diner. Pounding on the table he exclaimed, "COKE, NO PEPSI! THAT'S RICH! CHEESEBURGER, CHEESEBURGER, CHEESEBURGER! COKE, NO PEPSI!" THAT'S ONE OF MY FAVORITE SKITS ON SATURDAY NIGHT LIVE. REMEMBER THE DINER SKIT WHERE THE GUY BEHIND THE COUNTER WAS TAKING ORDERS AT THE HIS NUMBSKULL COUSIN WORKIN' AT THE GRILL, REPEATING WHAT WAS BEING YELLED OUT EVEN THOUGH IT WASN'T EVEN AN ORDER, THROWIN' MORE BURGERS ON THE GRILL UNTIL HE RAN OUT OF BURGER PATTIES?"

Jacob noticed that almost all noise in the diner had subsided as everyone was wide-eyed in amazement, looking toward where he was sitting. At that moment, he desperately wanted to crawl under the table and hide, feeling like all the stares from the room were directed at himself, a distinguished professor at the University who was having lunch with a loud, overbearing buffoon. D'Angelo, noticing that nobody else in the room, including Jacob, were not sharing in the humor, stopped laughing, let out a huge sigh, and said under his breath, "I guess you'd had to have been there."

Marci, still standing next to their table with a stunned expression, finally composed herself and commented, "I'll get this order in and get your food right out." She then turned and almost ran to the kitchen.

Slowly everyone in the diner dropped their stares and returned to the conversations they were having before the outburst and the diner noise returned to its previous level. Jacob's tension slowly subsided as the noise increased. Now he didn't feel like he was the center of attention any longer. As his attention was drawn back to D'Angelo, he again was having thoughts of just getting up and walking out of the diner to avoid any more embarrassment. However, he was quickly brought back to the moment by his tablemate.

"So, Doc, you always eat like a rabbit?"

"No, Mister D'Angelo, but at least when I eat, I'm not hearing the loud noises coming from my arteries slamming shut from all the fat and cholesterol."

"Hey, you're gonna die sometime, why not live for now? Excuse me for a minute; I'm gonna go wash my hands." D'Angelo got up from the table and started making his way through the crowded diner with the bunny ears on his slippers flopping as he walked along. Adding to Jacob's dismay and embarrassment, D'Angelo was stopping and conversing with diners as he was heading to his destination.

Watching what was happening; Jacob made the decision that it was time to leave. As he was getting ready to reach for his backpack and make his escape, he was startled by someone saying, "Doctor Prophitt, your lunch companion is quite the exuberant one, isn't he?" Jacob, recognizing the voice, slowly looked up to see Nathaniel Howard, the Dean of Students, standing next to the table and looking down at him through eyeglasses that he always wore sitting half way down his nose. Dean Howard was a short, rotund man with an obviously receding hairline and a bad "comb-over". Every time Jacob saw him, he was sporting a bow tie and wearing a combination of stripes and checks, looking more like a badly dressed car salesman than a school administrator.

Attempting to be scholarly in the Dean's presence, he calmly answered, "Yes Dean Howard, I do believe that he has a special zest for life, at least which is what I have found out in the short time that I have spent with him."

Dean Howard's eyes narrowed as he was still looking hard at Jacob; then he continued, "I do hope you have not forgotten about the 'Meet and Greet' at my home this afternoon. I think it would be wise for you to attend; it would be a good opportunity to meet more of your colleagues."

"Uh, yes Sir, I am planning on being there. It begins at two o'clock does it not?"

"That it does Doctor Prophitt. I look forward to seeing you there. I assume that you won't be bringing your *friend* along."

"Yes Sir . . . I mean, no Sir. I assure you that he will not be there."

"Good! I will see you then." Dean Howard turned on his heels and headed toward the exit. Jacob watched as he walked away, planning to get up and leave as soon as he went out the door; however, much to Jacob's dismay, he noticed that D'Angelo was navigating his way back through the tables and intentionally moving into the Dean's path. D'Angelo stopped Dean Howard, grabbed his hand, gave him an over-exaggerated handshake and laughed very loud after he had said something to him. The conversation ended and D'Angelo turned and continued toward his seat while Dean Howard looked at Jacob and gave him a hard look before turning and leaving the diner.

D'Angelo arrived at the table and sat down, "That guy seemed nice, but no sense of humor. I asked him for the name of his tailor and he didn't seem to like it very much."

"Mister D'Angelo, that *guy* is Nathaniel Howard, the Dean of students! He is over me in the teaching department. He deserves some respect!"

"Yeah, I know who he is, but it doesn't give him a license to have a lack of fashion sense."

Suddenly Jacob had a fire in his eyes and slammed his hands down on the table and leaned in toward his tablemate and said in a restrained, but angry voice, "Mister D'Angelo! Did you come here to observe me or to totally embarrass me in front of this whole community?"

As soon as he had spoken those words, Marci approached with their lunch. She set it in front of them and inquired, "Is there anything else I can get you gentlemen?"

D'Angelo removed the paper napkin from around his silverware and stuffed it down the front of his sweater, wearing it like a bib; he looked at the waitress and replied, "I'll need a bottle of ketchup please."

Marci smiled at him, "Sure thing, I'll bring it right away. Do you need anything Doctor Prophitt?"

With a scowl on his face, still glaring at D'Angelo, Jacob answered with an edge in his voice, "No thank you Marci, I'm fine."

D'Angelo lifted the top of the bun on his sandwich looking at what was under it, "You academia types take yourselves way too seriously. You need to lighten up . . . life's too short to not have a good laugh every once in a while."

Jacob plopped against the back of his chair putting his arms up in disgust. Just as he was ready to announce his departure from the diner, Marci returned with the ketchup, "Is there anything else I can get for you gentlemen?" With one of them still smiling and one still scowling, they both answered quietly by shaking their heads no. "Okay, wave me down if you decide you need anything else."

Lifting the bun off his burger, D'Angelo proceeded to smother his sandwich and the cheese-fries with ketchup. Looking over at Jacob he announced, "Now this is a well-balanced meal . . . protein, carbohydrates, and lots of red veggies. You better eat up Doc or your rabbit food will wilt on ya."

Jacob, still glaring hard at D'Angelo, sat up in his seat, reached for the container of salad dressing, put it up to his nose to smell it and poured the contents over the salad. He then picked up his fork and stabbed it into the center of his bowl picking up a large pile of lettuce. He held the fork up, pointing it at his lunch companion as he spoke, "Mister D'Angelo! I have had about all of you that I can take! You tell me that you are here to observe me . . . observe me for what? You show me a letter from the University, which I suspect is bogus, giving you permission to sit in on my sessions, and you manage to interrupt my entire class by snoring the entire time. Then you come to lunch parading around in floppy-eared bunny slippers, embarrassing me in front of my colleagues and this community. And, up to this point, you have yet to give me a real explanation of why you are here. Will you *please* tell me why you are here?"

D'Angelo took a huge bite out of his burger resulting in ketchup running down his chin. He picked up another napkin from the table, wiped off his chin and replied with a mouthful of food, "I told you Doc . . . my Boss sent me to observe you."

"Observe me for what Mister D'Angelo?"

"To see if you would fit in with my Boss' organization."

"And from all of this observing that you have been doing, what have you observed about me so far Mister D'Angelo?"

"Well, Doc . . . I've observed that you're wrapped pretty tight."

Jacob again sat back in his chair, laying the forkful of salad on his bowl, trying hard not to lose his composure. He watched D'Angelo stuff more cheese fries and hamburger into his mouth, appearing as if he had not eaten for several days. After a long, frustrating count to ten under his breath, Jacob mustered enough courage to engage in more conversation. "All right Mister D'Angelo, I will tell you that up to this point I have no interest in Cosmos something, something . . ."

"It's Cosmos Industries Unlimited, Doc."

"Yeah, like I said, Cosmos whatever, whatever. Based on their representation to me by you, I sincerely doubt that I would have an interest in joining your organization."

D'Angelo scooped up the last of the cheese fries with a fork and stuffed them into his mouth, then followed up with a napkin wiping up the excess cheese around his mouth. He chewed with a thoughtful expression on his face for a moment and then responded, "You know what Doc? You're right; I probably haven't done a very good job of representing my Boss. I have waltzed into your life not acting very professional. How about givin' me a Mulligan?"

"Mister D'Angelo, what the heck is a Mulligan?"

"It's a golf term Doc. Sometimes when you shank your tee shot into the trees, rather than going to find it, the guys you are playing with will give you a do-over. It's called a Mulligan. I'm asking for a do-over."

Jacob spoke again with a tone of sarcasm in his voice, "Okay Mister D'Angelo, being the fair and caring person that I am, knowing that you traveled a long way to get here, I will give you the benefit of the doubt and give you your 'Mulligan'. You can have my attention for a short time. I have a function to attend."

"Okay Doc, ask me anything you like. I'll try to answer your questions."

"Alright Mister D'Angelo, tell me about this Cosmos organization. What type of business do you do?"

"Doc, we are into everything. Mostly we work at making things here on Earth better for all mankind. The Boss is always creating new ways through his organization to provide the resources for his true love . . . feeding the hungry, caring for the needy, helping the oppressed and improving the environment. That's why he sends me to check out people like you, to see if you'd fit in."

After hearing the words D'Angelo had spoken, Jacob became slightly more interested in hearing about Cosmos. His posture changed and now he sat up attentively in his seat. "Mister D'Angelo, those are admirable qualities for an organization to have. So, is this a public company? Can I look you up on any of the stock exchanges or Google it to get more information?"

"No Doc, it's privately held. The Boss owns everything and runs the whole show with help from his Son and a field Advisor. Most everyone communicates with the Boss through the Son, except for a chosen few who answer directly to the Boss, and the Advisor assists the people in the organization with their decisions on a daily basis."

"Where is this organization located?"

"We are world-wide Doc."

"Mister D'Angelo, what I am asking is, are there any specific locations that this organization is operated from?"

"Like I said Doc, we are world-wide. We have satellite locations all around the world."

Jacob, now beginning to get frustrated again, feeling that D'Angelo was being evasive, tried to be more specific in his questioning, "Mister D'Angelo, what does this organization actually do? They must have an industry that provides revenue to accomplish all of these things you say your Boss strives to accomplish."

"Doc, all I can tell you is, if it exists, the Boss is probably involved in it somehow."

"If 'it' exists? What is 'it'?"

"Everything, Doc!"

"Mister D'Angelo! You are talking in circles! You mean to tell me that your Boss runs a world-wide company that is involved with 'everything', and he does this with help from just two other people? This sounds a little too farfetched to me."

"Doc, don't get me wrong . . . They have a lot of help from their associates around the world, but the Boss is an incredible guy. Between Him, His Son, and the Advisor, they act as a well-oiled machine. It's as if they are one."

"Mister D'Angelo, can you at least share with me the name of your Boss?"

"Sorry Doc, I'm not allowed to do that until you have been confirmed as a candidate."

"Mister D'Angelo, at the present time, I'm not sure that I am even interested in being a candidate!"

"Doc, that's your decision. We all have free will you know, but I do have a question for you."

"What is that Mister D'Angelo?"

"How you doin' in the faith department?"

Jacob's eyes narrowed and the scowl returned to his face as he asked a rhetorical question, fully knowing what was to come, "Mister D'Angelo, what are you asking me?"

D'Angelo leaned forward in his chair, looked up at the ceiling, and pointed his index finger up at the same time, "you know Doc . . . how ya doin' with the Man upstairs?"

Jacob instantly felt another surge of heat go up his spine, similar to the one he felt earlier in the day while talking with Rabbi Weiss. Choking back the anger in his voice, Jacob replied, "Mister D'Angelo, I am certain that there are State and Federal laws on the books that prohibit you from asking me about my religious beliefs. I take that as an insult and have no intention of answering that question!"

D'Angelo pulled out his notepad and pencil, licked the lead tip, and began writing something down. Jacob watched in silence for a moment, wondering what he was up to, until his curiosity forced him to ask, "What are you making a note of Mister D'Angelo?"

D'Angelo looked up from his notebook. "Well, Doc . . . I'm noting that you are questioning your faith."

Suddenly Jacob felt a great wave of anger and yelled out, "MISTER D'ANGELO! I DID NOT TELL YOU I AM QUESTIONING MY FAITH!" Suddenly Jacob could feel a lot of eyes staring at him. Even though the lunch crowd had thinned down, there were still several patrons in the diner who had heard his outburst, and it had gotten their attention. Jacob, now red-faced with embarrassment, leaned forward to get as close to D'Angelo's as possible remarked in a much quieter voice, "I did not give you an answer."

D'Angelo then leaned in closer to Jacob and spoke in almost a whisper, "Doc, you did give me an answer. My experience is that when I ask that question, the believers gladly answer me. People questioning their faith argue with me."

Jacob quickly sat back in his chair, stunned by the statement D'Angelo had just made. There was no denying what had been said; no rebuttal was possible. The embarrassment and anger just flowed out of Jacob leaving him spent, sitting quietly in his chair with almost no expression at all . . . just dumfounded.

"Doc, I gotta hit the road. I have an early tee time at Augusta National in the morning. It's a long drive from here, so if you have any more questions, ask now."

Jacob's mind was still swimming, feeling he had been blindsided by D'Angelo. Shortly, his faculties returned, "No Mister D'Angelo, I think you have answered all of my questions."

D'Angelo waived at Marci to get her attention. She quickly arrived at their table, still smiling, "What can I do for you gentlemen?" Just as D'Angelo was ready to talk, he expelled a huge belch, stunning both Jacob and Marci and probably several people sitting close by. With a chuckle, he responded, "Excuuuuuse me! I feel much better now!" He then released another hearty laugh, "It's time for me to get going, I need to pay the tab." D'Angelo reached into his pants pocket and pulled out a wadded-up mess of bills. Jacob could see a couple of hundreds and several tens and twenty-dollar bills, as well as ones in the wad. D'Angelo laid the whole wad in front of Marci, "Here, take out what you need for the bill and keep the rest. You did a great job; go treat yourself to something nice."

Marci was so stunned that her expression went blank and she turned pale, while at the same time her knees almost buckled and she steadied herself by putting a hand on the table.

As she regained her composure and her color returned, her smile came back even broader. Reluctantly pushing the wad back toward D'Angelo, "I can't accept that Sir. That's way too much money."

Immediately shoving it back toward Marci, D'Angelo urged, "Go ahead kid, I know you need the money. I insist!"

Marci stood motionless for a moment and her eyes kept growing wider the longer she looked at the wad of money in front of her, pondering whether it would be the right thing to do. Suddenly she blurted out, "Gee Mister . . . thanks a lot!" She quickly grabbed up the wad of money, like she was afraid D'Angelo would change his mind, stuffed it in her apron pocket and ran full speed back to the kitchen. Jacob watched Marci rush through the kitchen doors; then with a confused expression, he turned his attention back to D'Angelo.

D'Angelo, looking back at Jacob noticing his look, questioned, "What?"

Jacob did not answer for a minute, still trying to process what had just happened. Finally, he responded, "Do you have any idea how much money was in the wad you just gave that girl?"

D'Angelo scooted his chair back to get up from the table, "No not really. It doesn't matter anyway; I have an unlimited expense account. She's a student; I'm sure she can use the extra money." He stood up and started walking toward the exit.

Jacob grabbed his backpack and got up to follow D'Angelo out of the diner. As they walked out to the sidewalk, Jacob remarked, "Mister D'Angelo, you didn't even get a receipt."

"Yeah, I know, I'm bad about that. But hey, it's only money, and there's plenty more where that came from." D'Angelo stood on the walk next to the Mercedes as he pulled the wrapper off of a toothpick, which he had taken from the dispenser on the cashier's counter as he exited the diner. He put the toothpick in his mouth and stood there looking up at the mid-day sun. As he remained standing there, he appeared to be contemplating something; then he turned to Jacob and inquired, "So Doc, you a golfer?"

"I've tried to play a few times. I can't say that I have a passion for the game Mister D'Angelo."

"That's too bad Doc. To me, golf is a spiritual thing. I can't get enough of it."

"It appears you spend a lot of time at Augusta National Mister D'Angelo. Are you a member there? I understand it is a pretty exclusive club."

"Naw, I'm not a member, but I have a lot of connections, so I get to play there a lot. Have you ever been there Doc?"

"No, I haven't Mister D'Angelo. I have seen it on television when I have watched parts of the Masters Tournament. It looks like a beautiful place."

Suddenly D'Angelo had a far-off look in his eyes and a look of serenity on his face. He was quiet again for a few moments and then released a huge sigh, turned to Jacob, looking him squarely in the eyes, "Doctor Prophitt, it is probably the most beautiful place here on Earth; it is truly the portal to Heaven. When you stand on the thirteenth hole on a warm summer day with a slight breeze blowing across the fairway and the birds singing, you just know that God had a hand in creating that place."

Jacob was stunned, not only because D'Angelo had properly addressed him, but also because of the look of sincerity on his face while giving his description of the golf course. D'Angelo continued to stand quietly, staring off into the heavens for a few more moments. Then he abruptly announced, "Okay Doc, I gotta get goin'."

D'Angelo stepped off the curb, walked around to the driver's side of his car, and grabbed the door handle. He stopped as Jacob spoke up. "Mister D'Angelo, I do have one more question before you leave."

D'Angelo folded his arms on the top of the car, resting his chin on them, "Okay Doc, what is it?"

"Mister D'Angelo, you tell me that your Boss is passionate about the environment, but you are driving a big gas guzzler. How do you explain that?"

D'Angelo turned and started walking toward the back of the car. "Well, Doc . . . this isn't what you think it is. Come back here and let me show you something." He then stopped at the back of the car waiting for Jacob to join him. He pulled a key fob out of his pocket, pressed a button, and the motor roared to life. Squatting down behind the car, he motioned for Jacob to join him. Jacob stood near where D'Angelo was crouched down looking at him confused about what he was trying to show him. D'Angelo looked up at him. "Get down here and take a whiff of these exhaust fumes."

Jacob stepped back on the curb farther away from D'Angelo, beginning to think that he had lost his mind. "Mister D'Angelo, are you crazy? I don't make a practice of going around smelling gas fumes from auto exhaust pipes!"

D'Angelo began laughing. "Doc, I'm not crazy. These fumes are harmless. Come here, see and smell for yourself." Jacob, still thinking better of it, reluctantly stepped off the curb to join D'Angelo behind the Mercedes. He slowly crouched down, still wary of what he was about to do, and then put his nose near the exhaust pipe. Taking a sniff of the exhaust, at first being tentative, then he got closer and inhaled more of the exhaust. With an astonished look, he sat back on his heels gaping at D'Angelo. D'Angelo remained silent for a moment as he watched Jacob's expressions. "So, Doc, what do you think?"

Jacob, still in disbelief, replied, "Mister D'Angelo that smells like fresh mountain air. This is a top of the line, gas guzzling Mercedes, and its exhaust fumes smell like mountain air."

D'Angelo laughed at what Jacob said and continued, "That's nothin' Doc. Here, try this." He then cupped his hand under the exhaust pipe letting the condensation drip into his palm. After he had captured a few drops of the water, he put his hands up to his mouth, touching his tongue to the liquid. D'Angelo did not say anything, but just nodded at Jacob urging him to do the same thing.

Jacob, again being reluctant, slowly cupped his hand under the exhaust pipe collecting the condensation and then did as D'Angelo had done. After he had touched his tongue to the water, his eyes widened with amazement. "Mister D'Angelo, this tastes like spring water." He then stood up scrutinizing the long black automobile in front of him. "How are you doing . . . I mean, how is this possible?"

D'Angelo stood up, laughing again at Jacob's skepticism. He started walking around the car to the driver's side door. "It runs on water Doc. The Boss created it."

Jacob stepped back on the curb, walked around to the passenger side of the car, and then stopped and looked at D'Angelo from across the top of the car. "Mister D'Angelo, hydrogen technology is not a new creation. You are operating this on a hydrogen cell. That technology has been around for a while, and there's more and more of that being used every day. I don't believe this is something your *Boss* created."

"Doc I don't know anything about this hydrogen stuff you speak of, but there isn't any kind of cell on this car. All I know is that I fill the tank with a garden hose and it runs."

"Mister D'Angelo, you expect me to believe you run this thing on water from a garden hose? You must take me for some kind of fool."

"I'm not kiddin' Doc. In fact, it runs better on well-water. It must have a higher octane or somethin', so I usually stop and fill it up in the country."

"Mister D'Angelo, if this car actually runs on well-water, why hasn't your Boss introduced it yet, or is it still in research and development?"

"Nope Doc, it's been perfected. It's ready to go."

"Well then Mister D'Angelo, why hasn't it been brought to market yet? It would do wonders for the environment, not to mention the reduction of energy costs."

D'Angelo opened the car door getting ready to climb in, stopped and shot back, "Are you kiddin' Doc? The oil companies control the economy of the world. If the Boss was to introduce this now, it would probably get bought up by one of the oil companies and it would never see the light of day. Evil greed has a way of stopping good intent. It will get introduced when the Boss decides the time is right."

Jacob, still skeptical of the explanation he had just received, attempted to prod further for more proof. "Alright Mister D'Angelo, if you want me to believe this story of yours, why don't you raise the hood and let me see this miracle engine?"

"Sorry Doc, if I showed it to ya, I'd have to . . . well I'd rather not say. Hey, I gotta go!" He then slid into the driver's seat, closed the door and put the car in gear. Before he could pull away from the curb, Jacob rapped on the passenger side window trying to get his attention. D'Angelo hit the power window button lowering the passenger window, "What now Doc?"

"Mister D'Angelo, how do I get in touch with you, in case I have more questions?"

D'Angelo smiled, "Don't worry Doc; I have a feeling I'll be in touch with you very soon." He then closed the window and pulled away from the curb.

Jacob stood and watched as the Mercedes sped down the street, making a left turn at the first street it came to, disappearing from sight. He stood there for a long time lost in thought and absentmindedly glanced at his watch and felt a twinge of panic. Under his breath he exclaimed, "Oh shoot! I'm running late!" Then he quickly unlocked his bike, threw on his backpack, climbed on, and peddled down the street mulling over in his mind the weird day he had been experiencing already, hoping things would get back to normal . . . whatever normal was.

CHAPTER FOUR

JACOB FRANTICALLY PEDDLED DOWN THE street toward Dean Howard's home, grumbling under his breath as he traveled along. He was upset with himself for agreeing to have lunch with D'Angelo, which made him run late, causing him to have to change his plans to attend the 'Meet and Greet'. He had intended to go straight home from class, change into suitable attire for such a function, pull the tarp off Lizzie and drive there. Now that the early afternoon sun was out and the heat was up, he was concerned that not only was he going to be underdressed but also that he was going to smell like he had just run a marathon.

Turning onto Oak Street, Jacob noticed a residence with a large number of cars parked in the driveway and on the street in front of it; so, he figured that was his destination. Snaking his way between some cars he rode up onto the sidewalk. The front of the house had a broad wood-planked porch with large columns which made it look similar to a plantation mansion. The home sat on a rise above the street and there were several steps leading up to the front entrance. Not wanting to leave his bike at the street, he carried it up the steps and parked it at one end of the long porch away from the front door, not bothering to lock it up figuring he could at least trust the people that were part of the University's administration to not steal it.

After situating his bike, Jacob pulled a handkerchief from his pocket and wiped his brow of perspiration, trying to lower his level of frustration before making his entrance. He was certain he was going to walk into a party full of properly dressed people, while he was still wearing his safari ensemble, thanks to D'Angelo. Approaching the entrance, he peered through the sidelights of the doorway and could see people were milling around chatting, most having a glass of some sort of refreshment in their hands. He also noticed that all of the men he could see were attired in sport coats, just as he had planned to do. Finally mustering up the courage, he rang the doorbell. After what seemed like an eternity, the large, heavy wooden front door slowly swung open, making a long eerie creaking sound like you hear in all the horror movies just before some unsuspecting victim was just about to meet their doom. And there he was . . . the one-person Jacob didn't want to see at that moment.

"Well, Doctor Prophitt, I see you have finally blessed us with your presence. I'm glad to see that you dressed for the occasion." Taking a long hard look at Jacob and sticking his head out the front door and looking both directions, he continued, "I do hope you came alone."

"Oh . . . yes, Dean Howard, I am alone. I apologize for how I am dressed, but I was unfortunately detained and it made it impossible for me to go home and change before coming here."

"Don't pay attention to that ole fuddy-duddy!" Suddenly a short, very cheery, round-faced and somewhat rotund lady appeared, moving Dean Howard out of the way and sticking her hand out to greet Jacob. "I'm Jenny Howard. Please forgive Nathan. He gets all uptight at these University functions like it's important to be proper." She was an attractive lady with her blonde hair pulled up in a bun on top of her head and wearing a very flowery patterned Hawaiian muumuu. "As I recall, the invitation said casual attire, and so far, you are the only other person here besides me dressed accordingly."

Jacob managed a nervous little laugh. "Thank you, Misses Howard . . ."

Making a gesture by waving her hand in front of her, she replied, "Oh, please call me Jenny. I don't go much for that proper kind of stuff. I assume that you are the world-famous Doctor Jacob Prophitt that I have been hearin' all about."

"Yes ma'am, I wouldn't say world-famous, but that's me. Please call me Jacob."

"Well, Jacob, I think it's a great thing that you are here teachin' these kids. You're always welcome at our house; I don't care how you dress." Then she displayed another broad smile and the sincerity in her eyes reminded him of his Grandma Sarah, making Jacob feel much more at ease. "Now give me that heavy backpack and let me put it away for you while you join the party. Go get you a glass of iced tea. You look like you could use it."

"Thank you, Misses . . ." Suddenly she held up her index finger and shook it in the air giving him a reminder. "Uh . . . I mean Jenny."

"That's better. Just let me know when you are ready to leave and I'll get that back to you."

Jacob handed her his backpack and then proceeded to slowly wade into the sea of humanity. As he walked aimlessly through the room, people were sticking out their hands to shake his, announcing who they were and what department they were with. Jacob, just nodding and barely returning the pleasantries, was oblivious to all of it until he heard a familiar voice call out, "Hey, Jacob! Over here." Looking up, he saw the smiling face of Rabbi Weiss standing near, not surprisingly, the hors d'oeuvres table. Jacob seized the opportunity to find refuge from the crowd to be with somebody who was somewhat familiar, even though Aaron had been his first encounter to start out the bizarre day he had been experiencing.

Aaron held out his hand to shake Jacobs', "Bit overwhelmin', ain't it?"

"Yeah, I have to admit I wasn't looking forward to this. I didn't figure this many people would show up to this affair."

"Well, I tell ya what Jacob, y'all better get used to these gatherings. Dean Howard feels it's his duty to have these functions now and then to keep up the morale of the troops. The ones during the holidays are the best ones. I especially love the Christmas party." Aaron, laughing at his own humor, peered over the spread of food on the long table and picked up something that was unfamiliar to him, looked it over very carefully, sniffed it, and then popped it in his mouth. "I don't know what that was, but it was pretty good. So how was y'all's first day of teachin'?"

Jacob, still preoccupied with looking over the crowd and wondering how many people were crammed into the Dean's home, replied, "Well, Aaron, it went pretty well, outside of an unexpected interruption. Other than that, I think I can pull this thing off. From what I've received as feedback from the students, they seemed to enjoy the book I'm teaching from, so it should continue to go very well giving there are no more unforeseen circumstances."

"Oh, Jacob, ya can always count on the unforeseen circumstances. Just like right now, word is President Upton is lookin' for ya to have 'the talk'."

"The talk?"

Aaron put down the plate he was holding and put up his hands making an overly emphatic gesture like he was forming quotation marks, "Yeah, 'the talk'. He makes sure he meets face to face with every new professor that comes here so he can get to know them better."

Jacob was totally confused about what Aaron meant. "Okay . . . so what's the big deal about that?"

Aaron let out a little laugh. "Well, Jacob . . . y'all will just have to wait and see. Trust me, it's an experience like ya've never had before."

Jacob had just began feeling a little more at ease, but Aaron had managed to erase that temporary feeling of security and left him waiting for the other shoe to drop; and then it did. Jacob had just turned back toward the crowd to again survey the room when he noticed a tall, gray-haired gentleman, whom Jacob guessed to be in his early 70's, approaching him with his hand extended, obviously looking to shake another hand somewhere.

"Doctor Prophitt I assume. I've been waiting to make your acquaintance in person. Thank you for coming to this little soirée so we could meet." The gentleman was at least two inches taller than Jacob, and almost as slender. He spoke in a deep voice, well dressed sporting a perfect haircut, and had a very proper posture. He walked with long, purposeful strides and spoke with authority, leaving no doubt in Jacob's mind that this was the President of the University with whom he was about to have 'the talk'. Giving Jacob a stern handshake he continued, "Having been out of the country, unfortunately, I wasn't able to be directly involved with your recruitment; however, I must tell you I am delighted you chose to stay on and teach here at this institution."

"Thank you, President Upton. Those are kind words."

"Please, come join me for a while. I would like to have a face-to-face and get to know you a little better. Let's step out in the back yard and find a place to sit out by the stream. Misses Howard has created a beautiful oasis behind her home that is a site to behold."

Jacob followed President Upton as he walked toward the door to exit the room. As he was crossing the room, he could hear Aaron in the background saying, "Good luck Jacob." Looking back, Jacob saw him holding two thumbs up and sporting a big grin like a cat that just ate the canary.

The two men exited through the patio doors onto a large patio. At the edge of the patio there were steps which led down into what looked like an English garden, complete with all the hedges, greenery and flowers. It was something that one would expect to find behind one of the castles on the British Isles, only on a smaller scale. President Upton continued talking as they strode down a pathway; however, Jacob wasn't paying much attention to what he was saying as he was mesmerized by the 'Garden of Eden' which was totally hidden from the street out front. The home sat at the foot of one of the steep hills and there was a mountain stream that ran along the edge of the back yard with a sharp rise on the other side of the stream. Jacob was suddenly brought back to the moment when he heard, "How about here, Doctor Prophitt? Please, take a seat."

President Upton was standing next to a semi-circle of garden benches on a gray slate stone landing next to the bubbling water. Jacob immediately noticed the gentle breeze coming down from the mountain along the stream making the temperature at least ten degrees cooler than what it was while riding his bike out on the streets. President Upton continued, "This has to be one of my favorite locations in this whole community. There is always a cool breeze and the rippling waters of the stream are very calming. The Misses and I live across the street nearby. I love to come to the Howards' home and visit with them, sitting next to this stream, having conversations, and sipping wine. It's very good for the soul."

Jacob took a seat on one of the benches, still uncertain about what to expect, thanks to Aaron. He was feeling like maybe he should be fastening a seatbelt or something.

"So, Doctor Prophitt, we finally get to meet. Again, I apologize for not being personally involved with our recruiting efforts but, trust me, I was well-informed regarding all of the negotiations."

"Yes Sir . . . thank you Sir."

"I think it is a feather in the hat of the University when we get to procure one of our star students to return and teach the next generation of people who are stepping up to continue doing the work of God."

"Thank you, Sir . . . that's very kind."

"I trust that your living accommodations are sufficient."

"Uh . . . yes Sir. They will be fine for the time being. Thank you, Sir."

"Good . . . good, glad to hear that. I assume that your classroom situation is workable for you."

"Yes Sir, in fact I taught the first session today."

"Good . . . good."

President Upton became silent as his attention turned to a Blue Heron slowly wading down the stream, totally unconcerned about the humans sitting nearby. Jacob sat quietly as he fidgeted in his seat, uncertain about where the discussion was going to lead and President Upton looked as if his mind was far off in the distance. Suddenly, Upton snapped back to the present reality and continued, "I do hope, Doctor Prophitt that you fully understand the magnitude of your work here. These young people, somewhere in their lives, have made the decision to make a career out of spreading the good Word of our Creator, and there have been people in their lives who have influenced them to do so. When you step into a position such as you now have, you must realize that those who have influenced these youngsters have done the groundwork; you are now providing the capstone. You are essentially finishing a process; so, you need to be prepared to accept that responsibility."

"Uh . . . yes Sir. I understand Sir."

"These young people are taking on a huge task of teaching the Word, knowing from their own experience that is based on faith and, of course, the written Word provided to us by our Lord. But as a whole, faith still is the basis of what we believe. That is a difficult thing to convey to the non-believer, and sometimes even more so to those who just aren't sure of where they stand."

"Uh . . . yes Sir."

"As time goes on, when these students move into their chosen professions, they are going to experience all sorts of emotional ups and downs. They will experience the victories of bringing others closer to their faith and they will have to overcome the failures of attempting to convey their beliefs to those who just won't listen. They will have to deal with life, death, and even their own internal battles when they question their own faith. Trust me, Doctor Prophitt, there are going to be times when every one of them will be tested. Fortunately for many, their faith will be strong enough to carry them through; however, there are those few who will not be able to withstand the lies of Satan and will fall away from their faith."

"Yes Sir. I understand Sir."

"Doctor Prophitt, your thesis and the book that was published as a result of that thesis are true pieces of inspiration. I learned things about the prophets that I had never comprehended, even with all of my years of researching and teaching the Bible. Your words were truly a revelation to me, as I am certain they will also be a revelation to many others. Because of that, I felt it was in the best interest of the University to keep you on as a professor. You are the type of person that needs to be here forming our future soldiers for the war against Satan. You have a lineage, with both your father and grandfather being in the ministry; although I understand their methods of spreading the Word may be, or have been, somewhat unorthodox. Regardless of that, you were brought up in the ministry and you obviously have been blessed by our Lord with insight into the Word. We need you here to continue strengthening these young peoples' faith and give them a greater understanding of the history of our Christianity."

Jacob felt a knot beginning to form in his stomach as President Upton continued talking about faith and the importance of the work the University was doing. Thoughts about his own faith were drowning out President Upton's words. Jacob was looking right at him, but not hearing a word he was saying as he was questioning, in his own mind, why it had been so important to everyone he had met during this day that he believes in a God that may or may not exist. As long as he was correctly teaching what was written in the Bible, whether real or legend, and the students learned something from his teaching, what difference would that make? Jacob was snapped back to reality when he heard, "Doctor Prophitt, can I count on you?"

"Uh . . . sorry Sir . . . I was mulling something over for a moment. Could you please repeat the question?"

THE WORDS OF A PROPHITT

"Doctor Prophitt, I was asking you if I can count on you to be the person to prepare this next generation of teachers in the Word."

Jacob paused for a moment, not wanting to sound unsure with his answer. Sitting up straight, to give the appearance of confidence, he replied, "Yes Sir, President Upton! You can count on me." Then, suddenly, the knot returned to his stomach, the same knot that he felt every time he fibbed to Grandma Sarah when he was a little boy.

"Good . . . good, I'm glad to hear that. I knew we had made the right choice when we decided to create this position for you. So, Doctor Prophitt, I've been doing all the talking. Is there anything I can answer for you?"

"Yes Sir, there is something I have on my mind. Are you familiar with a Michael D'Angelo?"

Suddenly a huge smile came across President Upton's face and he gave a hearty laugh before answering. "Ah yes, my good friend Michael. He's a card, isn't he?"

"Uh . . . yes Sir, he is that. He visited my classroom today and I wasn't sure if that was something that was authorized."

President Upton continued to laugh to himself as he was still thinking about D'Angelo, "Oh yes Doctor Prophitt . . . I can assure you that the visit was authorized. I signed the letter of authorization myself. You know, it would behoove us all to be more like Michael, a little more carefree." President Upton became quiet again for another moment as if lost in a thought and then continued, "Doctor Prophitt have you ever been to the Isle of Patmos?"

"Uh . . . no Sir, I have not visited Patmos."

"Well . . . Misses Upton and I visited there recently, and I must tell you it was a revelation. I became interested in visiting the place when I was knocking around the University library one day and found a book that was written by a chap from England. His name was Peter France. He was Oxford educated and worked as a journalist over there. He talked about his transformation from not believing in the Lord to becoming a follower of Christ. He had struggled with his faith throughout his life, even after experiencing his wife having a medical miracle that she attributed to prayer; he still wasn't a believer. Then something amazing happened. He and his wife took a trip to Patmos and he immediately became enamored with the people there. He was amazed at how they reveled in their religious festivals, and their zeal for their faith in Christ. He was taken aback at how the ouzo flowed and the people ate and danced to celebrate. It was a far cry from the stodgy, straight-laced attitude he experienced as a child going to church in England. So, Doctor Prophitt, do you get up and dance in the aisle in church during the hymns?"

"Uh . . . no Sir, I can't say that I do."

"Well you should. Anyway, as I was telling you, this France fellow was very intelligent. He began visiting one of the centuries old churches on Patmos, and there were tomes of religious writings. He actually taught himself to read the Greek language and began reading some of those books. He came across the Greek translation of the Gospel of John, and once he read that he was hooked. The words written by Saint John struck him so deeply that he became a believer. Isn't that an amazing story Doctor Prophitt?"

"Uh . . . yes Sir, it is an amazing story."

"So, as I was telling you, after reading that book by Mister France, I put visiting Patmos on my so-called bucket list; and I must tell you that everything Mister France wrote about that place is true. Those people really know how to revel in their Lord. You know, in the Bible it tells us to make a joyous noise for the Lord. We are meant to celebrate our faith joyously! Why even King David danced naked before the Ark of the Covenant, much to the chagrin of Bathsheba, while it was being delivered to Jerusalem. Most of us white folk sit around quietly in our pews in church singing some of those old southern gospels talking about the joy of our Lord, making them sound like funeral dirges. Somewhere in our history it almost became a sin to sing in church. Why I remember one of our former students telling me that a church he attended up in Indiana took up a collection and bought their first organ sometime back in the early nineteen-hundreds. Sadly, one of the parishioners was so upset about it he took an ax and destroyed the organ. Isn't that crazy Doctor Prophitt?"

"Uh . . . yes Sir . . . that is crazy."

"I tell you Doctor Prophitt; those people on Patmos celebrate until they drop. It is the most amazing thing I have ever witnessed, and it has changed my perspective on what our faith in the Lord is all about." Then again, President Upton went silent, gazing off into space as if he wasn't even on the planet. Jacob nervously remained quiet not wanting to disturb Upton's train of thought. Eventually Upton returned to earth, "I'm sorry Doctor Prophitt, what were we discussing before I got on this tangent about Patmos?"

"Mister D'Angelo Sir."

"Ah yes . . . Michael. Are you a golfer Doctor Prophitt?"

"Uh . . . no Sir, I have tried it a few times, but I didn't play very well."

"Well . . . Doctor Prophitt, golf is one of my passions and that is one thing Michael and I have in common. Let me warn you now, don't ever play him for money. He will start out on the first couple of holes slicing the ball and hitting roughs and sand traps and then he will entice you to play for money." President Upton paused for a little chuckle and then continued, "Once you agree to bet, his ball suddenly acts like it has a guidance system. He can make some of the most miraculous shots you have ever seen. He is a true golf hustler . . . mark my words."

"Uh . . . yes Sir, I would agree he's a hustler."

"Did he mention to you that he golf's most of the time at Augusta National, where they play the Masters tournament?"

"Yes Sir, he did mention that to me."

"Michael has promised me he will take me down to Augusta so I can play a round on that famed golf course sometime in the near future." President Upton again gazed off into space for a moment and then let out a huge sigh, "Oh, Doctor Prophitt . . . that will be a glorious day indeed." President Upton continued his quiet gaze for a while longer and then abruptly stood up from his seat extending his hand to Jacob. "Doctor Prophitt, it has been a real pleasure conversing with you. I feel as if I know you much better after our little talk. I hate to rush off, but I must get back to the house and mingle a little longer before I leave."

Jacob arose from his seat and shook President Upton's hand, too stunned to say a word.

"Doctor Prophitt, if you ever need anything, please do not hesitate to visit my office. My door will always be open for the University's star professor. Have a blessed day."

Jacob was still not able to respond as President Upton turned and walked down the pathway toward the house where the party was still underway. He watched Upton as he strolled along, humming something that sounded a lot like 'Amazing Grace', stopping every few steps to smell a flower or look at a plant before continuing on. When President Upton disappeared around a bend in the path, Jacob sat back down on the bench. Looking across the stream, he noticed the Blue Heron still standing motionless looking back at him. Then,

THE WORDS OF A PROPHITT

as if the bird would understand, Jacob spoke to it, "What the heck was that all about?" The Heron appeared to wink back at Jacob, shook its head, majestically extended its wings, leapt up and took flight heading up stream. As Jacob watched the bird fly away, he replied under his breath, "Yeah, just what I thought. You don't believe it either."

CHAPTER FIVE

A FTER PRESIDENT UPTON HAD LEFT, Jacob sat by the stream for a few more moments, trying to grasp what had occurred during the odyssey he was experiencing, that had begun earlier in the day. Wanting to find a sanctuary from the ongoing barrage of discussions about his faith, he decided to head for home. Returning to the party, he attempted to wade through the crowd as quickly as he could, still having to stop and respond to the greetings of people he had yet to meet. Noticing Rabbi Weiss still standing next to the hors d'oeuvres table across the room, Jacob decided not to take the time to converse with him, but rather, gave him a wave indicating that he was leaving. Finally, he was able to track down Jenny Howard to retrieve his backpack. After giving her a lame excuse for leaving early, he exited out the front door of the home, picked up his bike, carried it down the steps, climbed on and started peddling frantically down the street.

After traveling a few blocks, feeling like he had escaped the crowd, Jacob slowed his pace and peddled at a leisurely speed. As he rode along rehashing the day, the farther he traveled the more irritated he became. After what seemed to him like an eternity, riding in the late afternoon heat toting a heavy backpack, he finally arrived home and rode into the driveway. Dismounting, he walked the bike into the detached garage and placed it along the wall next to Lizzy. While standing in the shade cooling off and gathering his thoughts, he looked out the side door and noticed all of his girls jumping around in the back yard. The two older girls, Bethany and Ruth, were somewhat in unison with their moves, but the three younger girls were jumping around to the beat of another unheard drummer. Assuming they were practicing cheerleading, Jacob forced out a little smile and walked out into the yard and called out, "Hi girls! Whatever you are doing, you look good doing it."

Almost in unison, five girls yelled out, "HI DADDY!" They all ran over to give Jacob a group hug . . . something that happened each time he would return home after being away, even if it was just to the grocery store for five minutes. After everyone released their hug, Bethany asked, "How was your first day at work Daddy?"

Jacob felt like blurting out what he really felt, but instead answered, "It was very interesting. I will tell you about it sometime."

Bethany appeared to ponder his response for a moment, and then replied, "Okay." She then turned on her heels, with her four sisters in tow, and returned to the spot where they had been doing their cheers. Jacob watched them for another moment, smiled and shook his head, then walked toward the house.

Entering the doorway from the back yard into the kitchen, he ran into Rebecca who was still dressed in her nursing scrubs, standing directly inside the door to greet him. Rebecca was tall in her own right, just over five foot ten and almost as slender as Jacob. Her red hair was natural and her skin was the creamy white that you would expect from a true red head. Still having a girlish figure and with her hair pulled back in a pony tail, she looked like she could still pass for a college coed; however, Jacob's salt and pepper hair made him look much older than he was. The two had met in high school and were immediately attracted to each other partially because they were both so tall. He didn't have to stoop over to kiss her and she wasn't self-conscious about being taller than the guy she was with, which was the case with most boys in her class. As time went on, their friendship transformed into love, and the rest is history.

Jacob gave Rebecca a quick kiss on the cheek and then barged around her to the kitchen sink and began to wash his hands, blurting out, "Man . . . you wouldn't believe the day I've had!" He didn't notice that Rebecca was making contorted facial expressions, trying to get his attention without saying anything out loud. He continued, "Right off the bat, I am greeted by a Rabbi dressed like a nineteen eighties Yuppie, who apparently was so wired on coffee that he wouldn't even take a breath between sentences. And not only that, his accent was so strong you could tell he's from the deep South."

Suddenly his tirade was interrupted when Rebecca yelled out, "JACOB!" Startled, Jacob looked at his wife, who was tilting her head toward the hallway door, trying to get him to notice something. "We have a visitor."

Then Jacob heard a strange voice, also in a southern accent say, "Hi, I'm Mindy Weiss. I'm married to that wired Rabbi that ya'll are speakin' of." Jacob turned back from Rebecca to look out the window over the sink at the back yard; frozen like a statue, he felt his face turning three shades of red from embarrassment. He then took a deep breath and slowly turned around to find a short lady standing behind him who had almost the same build as Rabbi Weiss. She had short dark hair and sported a huge smile. She let out a big laugh, "Don't ya just hate it when that happens?" Then she grabbed Jacob and gave him a bear hug that seemed to Jacob to last forever. Rebecca was obviously enjoying the whole thing as she was bent over laughing hysterically.

Jacob finally recaptured his composure while Mindy was still hugging him, "I am so sorry. That was rude of me."

Mindy broke her hug, still laughing, "Don't give it a second thought. Y'all described Rabbi Weiss to a tee. He gets nervous 'bout things and then drinks too much coffee and turns into a babblin' Georgian. He's been talkin' 'bout meetin' you fer days so I knew this was comin'. Anyway, I've gotta go. Y'all are gonna be gettin' ready for dinner. It's been really nice meeting y'all."

Rebecca bent over to give Mindy a hug, "Thank you for stopping by. I feel much better about Ezekiel's school now that I know you are his teacher."

Mindy returned the hug and headed for the door. "Oh, it's my pleasure. I'll watch over the lil' guy like he's my own." She started out the door, stopped, turned around and asked, "So Jacob . . . was Aaron eatin' fruit when ya saw him this mornin'?"

Being put on the spot, Jacob stammered, "Well . . . uh . . ."

"And when ya were at the party, was he stayin' near the food table?"

"Well . . . uh . . ."

"Just what I thought; I'm gonna punch him right in the throat and make him hike ten miles when he gets home. He's supposed to be on a diet with me!" Then she let out another hearty laugh and left the house through the back door.

After a few moments of tense silence, Rebecca spoke up, "Wow! That was embarrassing. It's a good thing you didn't say everything you were thinking." Then she started laughing again at Jacob. Sensing that he was getting angry with her, she went over and kissed Jacob on the cheek and gave him a hug, "Oh Honey, you take things way too seriously. Trust me; you didn't hurt Mindy's feelings. In the short time I've spent with her, I'm pretty sure she wasn't offended. I think everything is funny to her."

Jacob, not feeling very reassured broke away from Rebecca and returned to the window to look out at the back yard where the girls were still jumping around. "So, what are the girls doing?"

Rebecca moved over next to Jacob, put her arm around his waist, laid her head on his shoulder and gave him an affectionate hug while looking out the window with him. "Bethany has been invited to try out for the freshman class cheerleading squad, so she's practicing and the other girls are helping her out."

Jacob broke out laughing, "I don't think Bethany is getting a whole lot of help out there. It looks more like a poorly orchestrated monkey ballet." After a moment of contemplating Rebecca's comment, he turned to her, "I'm not sure I like the idea of Bethany being out in front of a bunch of people jumping around in a little cheerleading outfit, especially in front of a bunch of teenage boys with their hormones raging."

Rebecca turned back to Jacob and put her arms around his neck, giving him a long kiss; then she pulled away giving him a wink. In an attempt to use her alluring voice, she commented, "As I recall, you didn't mind me jumping around in my little volleyball outfit when we were in high school." She turned and walked toward the refrigerator with an exaggerated swing in her walk, trying to look seductive but giggling at the same time.

Jacob tried to argue the point, "That's not the same thing. This is our daughter we are talking about."

THE WORDS OF A PROPHITT

Rebecca had her head stuck in the refrigerator looking for something to make for the evening meal. Not finding anything at the moment, she stood up and looked at Jacob, "Well, if you remember Mister Prude, I was somebody's daughter also."

"Yeah, well I don't . . ." Then Jacob's words trailed off knowing he was in an argument he had no chance of winning. Still standing at the kitchen window watching the girls, he was thinking to himself how Bethany was becoming the spitting image of her mother and wondering how in the world she had suddenly turned into a teenager; where had the time gone? Then it dawned on him that he had four more daughters coming up behind Bethany. He began thinking that he needed to build a castle with a moat and high walls around it to keep out all of the boys that were going to be hanging around trying to get to his daughters as they got older and prettier.

"JACOB!"

Startled back to reality, he turned to look at Rebecca. "What? I'm sorry, what did you say?"

"So, how about I order in pizza? I don't feel like cooking anything tonight."

"Uh sure, that sounds good. By the way, where's Zeke? I haven't seen him since I got home. He's usually hanging around with the girls."

Rebecca looked at Jacob with a concerned expression. "Zeke's up in his room. He came home from school really congested and tired. I think the pollen counts are up and it really hit him. I gave him some medicine to help him out. You know how it knocks him out when he takes that stuff. The last time I checked on him he was lying on his bed playing on his Game Boy."

Jacob, still watching the girls in the backyard, responded, "I guess I had better go up and check on the little guy." Turning away from the window he headed for the stairway, stopping to put his hand on Rebecca's shoulder, giving her a reassuring look. Rebecca gave him a meek smile and then started dialing the phone to order supper as Jacob climbed the stairs to Ezekiel's room.

Once Jacob reached the door to the bedroom, he paused and smiled at the signs that had been posted on the door that read 'Stay Out' and 'Danger, Enter at Your Own Risk', obviously trying to scare his sisters from going into his room. Because of Ezekiel's condition, the University had their maintenance crew convert an attic area into another bedroom where the two older girls could sleep; leaving the younger three girls in one of the regular bedrooms so Ezekiel could have his own.

Jacob entered the room and immediately noticed the familiar strong odor of Vicks VapoRub coming from the humidifier that was used to make Ezekiel's breathing easier when he was congested, which happened a lot during the summer and fall seasons. Ezekiel was on his bed sitting up with his back against pillows that were propped up against the headboard. He was still dressed in his school clothes playing on his handheld computer, even though it appeared that his eyes were half closed from drowsiness.

"Hey buddy, how are you feeling?"

Ezekiel looked up at Jacob and his eyes opened a little wider. Suddenly he began coughing and Jacob could hear the rattling of the mucus that had built up deep in his son's lungs. When Ezekiel's coughing subsided, he weakly answered, "I'm okay."

Jacob walked over to the skinny little freckle-faced boy, brushed his red hair back and gave him a kiss on the forehead, not only to show his love but also to see if his son had a fever. Jacob continued to be amazed at how Ezekiel would never complain, no matter how bad he felt. The answer was always the same, "I'm okay."

Sitting down on the edge of the bed and reaching for the trusty plastic bowl and bottle of water that were kept close by on the nightstand, Jacob inquired, "So Zeke, how about I beat on you a little and see if we can get some of that yucky stuff out of you?"

"Okay." Laying down his computer, Ezekiel crawled across the bed and lay across Jacob's lap, resting his chin on his crossed arms. With the edge of his hands, Jacob began lightly beating up and down on Ezekiel's back. This was a procedure that the doctors suggested Jacob use to help Ezekiel bring up the mucus in his lungs, so he could breathe easier.

Jacob began the usual line of questioning he did while he was working on his son, "So did you have a good day at school?"

"It was okay." When Ezekiel answered it sounded like he was talking through a fan as Jacob was beating on his back.

"Do you like your new teacher, Misses Weiss?"

"Yeah, she's nice."

"Did you learn anything new today?"

"Yeah, I guess so."

"What did you learn?"

"I don't remember."

"I would think if you learned something you would remember it."

"Yeah, I guess so."

"So, did you find a new girlfriend at school today?"

With that question, Ezekiel raised his head, looked back at his father and with more emotion than he had shown until now, answered, "Oh Daddy, you're being silly. I don't care about girls yet. I'm too young."

Jacob smiled to himself, happy that he at least had gotten a little bit of emotional response from Ezekiel. "Oh Zeke, you're never too young to care about girls. Being a cute little red-headed guy like you are, you're going to have them chasing after you all the time."

"OH . . . YUCK DADDY!"

With that little outburst, Ezekiel began coughing; Jacob could tell that something was beginning to move deep down in his chest. Both of them knew the drill . . . Jacob reached for the bowl and Ezekiel moved his head to the edge of the bed, getting situated over it. After a few deep coughs the mucus started coming up. Ezekiel sounded like he was gagging; however, the 'yucky stuff' was breaking loose and he started spitting it into the bowl, while Jacob continued to lightly pat him on the back. After a short time, the gagging subsided and Ezekiel stopped coughing and the tension in his body eased up. He lay quietly as Jacob gently massaged his back, knowing that his son was done bringing up the mucus. After resting there for a while, Ezekiel rolled off of Jacob's lap, picked up the bottle of water laying on the bed, took a couple of swigs from it before he lay back on his pillows, obviously worn out.

Jacob picked up the bottle and placed it back on the nightstand next to Ezekiel's bed. "Mom ordered pizza and it should be here in a little while. Are you hungry?"

Ezekiel reached for his Game Boy and immediately focused on the game he had been playing. "I guess so. I'm going to play my game until it gets here . . . okay?"

"Sure . . . let me get this stuff out of here." Jacob picked up the bowl, left Ezekiel's room and went to the bathroom across the hall to clean things up. After emptying the bowl and rinsing it out, he returned to Ezekiel's bedroom to find him sound asleep, with his Game Boy still clutched in his hands. Jacob gently pulled the toy out of his son's grasp and laid it on the nightstand and reached for a blue and white afghan which lay across the end of the bed and pulled it up across Ezekiel. The afghan was knitted for him by his Great Grandma Sarah when he was born; it was usually the first thing he wanted when he wasn't feeling well.

Jacob sat on a chair next to the bed and watched his son sleeping. It looked like he was resting comfortably, but there was still the sound of the rattling deep down in Ezekiel's lungs. As he was watching his son, Jacob's eyes started to well up. Close to having full blown tears, Jacob bowed his head and clasped his hands together and sat quietly for a few moments. Then he spoke in a whisper, "God . . . if you do exist, why would you do this to my only son?" He continued to sit quietly, with tears starting to roll down his cheeks, until his thoughts were interrupted by the sound of the doorbell ringing. Knowing that the pizza must have arrived, he sat back in his chair to wipe away the tears and get his emotions under control before going back downstairs to be with the rest of the family. After a few more moments, Jacob took a deep breath, stood up, and exited Ezekiel's room, quietly closing the door so he wouldn't disturb him.

Entering the kitchen, Jacob saw Rebecca and Bethany busy setting the kitchen table for supper; the younger girls were all jockeying for sink time to wash their hands getting ready to eat, giggling as they nudged each other out of the way. Rebecca watched them with a smile on her face. "Why don't a couple of you young ladies use the hall bath, so you can all get washed up?" The two youngest, Esther and Martha broke away, running down the hallway with Esther in the lead yelling, "I'M FIRST!" They both made it to the bathroom door together, still pushing each other and giggling as they made their way in to wash their hands.

    Jacob stood quietly watching and listening to all the activity and enjoying all of the happy banter that was occurring. However, at the same time he felt sad that Ezekiel couldn't be there to join in. Rebecca looked up and noticed him, "Where's Zeke? Is he feeling better?"

    "He'll be okay. He fell asleep, so I thought I would let him rest for a little while. I am sure he will be up shortly. He knew that pizza was coming, and you know how much he likes pizza."

    Rebecca gave Jacob a somber smile and continued to finish up the place settings while Bethany sat the pizzas on the table. "Okay girls, let's get finished up so we can sit down and eat before supper gets cold." Almost simultaneously, all the girls arrived, scooting chairs around to get seated at the table. Soon all the commotion turned to silence and everyone, including Jacob, held the hand of the one next to them. After Rebecca was sure everything and everyone was ready, she announced, "Okay Esther, I think it's your turn for the blessings tonight."

    Everyone at the table knew this would take a while, as Esther was the wordy one in the family. After a long prayer in which she asked for healing for her brother Zeke, and blessing everything and everyone from her hamster to the pizza delivery boy, she finally finished. Then everyone at the table ended the prayer with an exaggerated "Amen!" All at once the girls started laughing, reaching for pizza, and talking at the same time about the day's events. Jacob and Rebecca sat quietly, smiling lovingly at each other from across the table, absorbing all the repartee occurring, before filling their own plates. When everyone started biting into the food, the conversation became less frequent, and the room became quieter.

Soon after the meal began, Ezekiel quietly stumbled into the kitchen, looking like he was still half asleep, carrying his Game Boy and dragging his afghan along with him. Everyone became silent as he crawled into the chair next to Rebecca, his usual place to sit at the table. As he lay his head against his mother, she put her arm around him and gave Ezekiel a kiss on top of his head. "Are you feeling better?"

"I'm okay."

"Are you hungry?"

"Yeah . . . a little."

"Are you still asleep?"

"Yeah . . . a little."

The quiet at the table suddenly ended as all the girls erupted into laughter at Ezekiel's response. Rebecca gave Ezekiel a hug, removed her arm from around his shoulders and placed some pizza on his plate. Then the evening meal with all in attendance continued.

When everyone was finished eating, Rebecca announced, "Okay kids, it's time to clean up the table and get started on your homework." As usual, that garnered a few moans and groans, but everyone got up from the table and completed their assigned tasks. When everything was cleaned up, the family reconvened at the table, including Jacob and Rebecca. Homework in the Prophitt household had become a team effort, with everyone helping. The older girls would help the younger girls and Ezekiel, while Jacob and Rebecca would help as needed. As each one completed their schoolwork, they were allowed a little more playtime before they had to get their clothes ready for the next day and prepare to go to bed.

When all their homework was finished, the children disappeared to wherever they would go to get away from their parents. Jacob and Rebecca grabbed their evening glass of iced tea and convened on the back porch to listen to the songs of the evening birds and watch the sun begin to sink below the mountains in the west. After a few moments, Jacob broke the silence, "I looked at the weather for the weekend and it's supposed to be clear. I think I'm going to take Lizzy on a road trip and visit Grandpa Eli. He's been on my mind a lot lately; I feel like I need to get over to Somerset and check on him. I don't have another session until mid-week, so I have plenty of time."

Rebecca sat in silence, not moving a muscle as she watched the sunset. Jacob was feeling uneasy since she wasn't responding, so he decided to keep quiet until she did. After what seemed like an eternity, Rebecca swallowed the last of her tea, stood up from her seat, moved over and kissed Jacob on the forehead. "I think that would be a good idea. The kids and I are working at the Church bazaar this weekend. That will give me a good excuse for you not being there when people ask me why the celebrated author of 'The Words of the Prophets' is not there helping out. I need to go in and check on the kids." With that said, she entered the house leaving Jacob all alone with his thoughts. He hated when she did that. His refusal to attend church had created an undercurrent of tension between them which would usually lay dormant until moments like this. When the subject would come up, Rebecca could usually find a way to casually stick in the dagger and give it a twist.

Suddenly, Rebecca stuck her head out the back door, "Oh, by the way, I forgot to tell you there is a message on the voicemail from a Lucinda? She says she works for someone called Diablo Publishing? She said she needs to talk with you about your future projects. It's still on there . . . I didn't erase it."

THE WORDS OF A PROPHITT

Jacob nodded his acknowledgement rather than doing it verbally, still stinging from Rebecca's comment a few moments earlier. Jacob thought to himself, "Who the heck is Lucinda, and how the heck did she get our phone number? I thought it was unlisted."

The sun was now almost entirely behind the mountains and it was becoming dusk. Jacob noticed something out of the corner of his eye that caught his attention. Looking up the steep hill that was at the edge of their yard, he noticed a glow that appeared to be a campfire in a clearing that was probably a hundred feet above the house. Jacob was familiar with that site on the hill since he had visited it on many occasions. The clearing was accessible via an old fire trail that Jacob would take his bike on while riding in the hills. When he was there, he could look down over the house and yard from high above, seeing everything that was going on in their yard and the neighborhood around them. Speculating that it was probably some of the students out doing a little celebrating, he hoped they were intelligent enough to get back to campus before it got too dark and the mountain wildlife, namely the bears, started foraging for food.

Deciding to call it an evening, Jacob got up from his chair and headed for the door to enter the house. He stopped for a moment and took a deep breath before going in, knowing that it was probably going to be a chilly evening at the Prophitt house.

CHAPTER SIX

JACOB STEPPED OUT ONTO THE back stoop of the house carrying a duffle bag packed with his traveling necessities, stopping to inhale the fresh air and check the sky for rain clouds before heading to the garage. The weather man had changed the forecast to a chance of rain, but it looked like it was going to be another perfect autumn day. It was warm with a lot of sunshine and the trees on the surrounding mountains were just beginning to change to their fall colors.

Jacob was now alone as he watched Rebecca and the kids pull out of the driveway headed to the church bazaar. He had stayed until they were loaded up and, on their way, so it was time to hit the road on his way to Grandpa Eli's. Entering the garage, Jacob set his bag down, walked over to the car, and grabbed a corner of the tarp that covered it. He gingerly rolled it up as he removed it from the prized possession that was hidden underneath. Once the tarp was completely removed, Jacob stood back and began his inspection of Lizzy, a nineteen sixty-six, British racing green, Austin Healey Mark III. It was a car that had been purchased many years ago on a whim by his Grandpa Eli and Grandma Sarah.

The family lore was that one time while the grandparents were on tour with their traveling gospel show, the caravan had stopped at a diner just outside of Shreveport,

Louisiana. Sarah saw the car sitting on a car dealer lot across the street from where they were eating. She became so enamored with the green color, the bug-eye headlights and the grill that looked as if the car had a gigantic smile, that she was unable to take her eyes off it. When they had finished their lunch, Eli and Sarah walked hand in hand to the lot, just to look at it . . . so they thought. After taking a quick test drive and talking it over for a few minutes, they found themselves signing the paperwork, writing a check and driving the car for the rest of the tour. Thinking the car should have a proper English name since it was built in Great Britain, Sarah dubbed her 'Elizabeth'. Somehow as time went by, the name was shortened to 'Lizzy', and Sarah would harshly reprimand anyone who would absentmindedly call her 'Tin Lizzy'. She was quick to remind them that there was no 'tin' in 'Lizzy'. Eli always claimed that Lizzy was their one true indulgence in life.

Often when their grandparents were home in the off-season from their tour, the grandchildren would get to take rides in the car on the winding roads around Somerset, Kentucky with Grandma Sarah behind the wheel. Jacob, having lived with his grandparents during his teens, had spent the most time in the car. When Sarah passed, the car sat idle and Eli eventually lost interest in having Lizzy sitting in the barn reminding him of Sarah every time he went in to get something. So, he decided to hand it down to Jacob rather than selling it to someone who wouldn't appreciate the car's history with the family. Lizzy had fallen into disrepair, so Eli and Jacob's father, David, pooled their resources and had the car restored to her original condition. Once she was completed, Jacob's father and grandfather awarded her to Jacob in recognition of earning his doctorate degree.

Jacob took a soft feather duster off a hook on the wall of the garage and began to gingerly remove the thin layer of dust Lizzy that had gathered on her under the tarp while sitting idle in the garage. He began the inspection routine that Eli had taught him to follow, much like a pre-flight routine that pilots use before taking off in their airplanes. He raised the bonnet to check the oil, hoses, and all the fluid levels, giving everything in the engine compartment a quick look-over. Then he took an air gauge out of the glove compartment to make sure there was proper air pressure in all the tires. After a quick test of all the headlights and tail lights, being convinced everything was in proper working order, Jacob grabbed his duffle bag and placed it in the trunk, or rather the 'boot' in British lingo. He then lowered the convertible top, crawled behind the wheel, fired Lizzy up, and backed her out of the garage, stopping to let her idle so the engine would warm up. While he was waiting for the engine heat gauge to register the prescribed temperature of one-hundred sixty degrees Fahrenheit, he adjusted the mirrors and then reached for his tartan, British ivy cap in the passenger seat, pulling it onto his head with his ponytail sticking out of the back of it. Donning his sun glasses, he looked very much like an English gentleman prepared to go on 'holiday' with a drive across the British Isle . . . maybe to the shores of Scotland.

Once all systems indicated "go", Jacob put Lizzy in reverse, backed out of the driveway onto the street, drove to the edge of town and turned onto the narrow road that was the main access to outside civilization, heading toward Somerset, Kentucky. This was a trip that Jacob had made before in Lizzy, taking the scenic route staying on the two-lane highways that snaked through the Smoky Mountains traveling west. The route that he had carefully mapped out was calculated so he would not be too far from any of the small towns that dotted the way for any long stretches of time. Driving an almost fifty-year-old car could be an adventure, not knowing what might break down at any given moment.

The first leg of the trip was the most mountainous, and the most fun for Jacob, as the road had a lot of steep climbs and downhill runs as well as tight curves. Thus, this created a lot of gear-changing, accelerating and braking, giving Jacob an opportunity to put the 'old girl' through her paces. Eli often reminded Jacob that this was a car built to be driven, not coddled. After being on the road for more than an hour, the hills and curves became less frequent and the job of driving Lizzy had become less action-packed.

With the straighter and flatter road ahead, Jacob had more time to view the scenery and reflect on his life, both past and present. His honest justification to Rebecca for the trip was that he wanted to check on his grandfather's well-being. In recent phone conversations with Eli, Jacob had gained a sense that his grandfather was giving up. During those calls Eli wasn't his usual jovial, full-of-life self. It concerned Jacob that his grandfather was living alone at eighty-eight years of age in a rural area outside of Somerset. He had no family nearby, or even in the same state for that matter, and the closest neighbor resided almost a quarter-mile from him. But Eli was adamant that he was doing alright, and he wasn't about to be a burden on anyone.

While that was all true, Jacob had an even bigger ulterior motive. He wanted to unearth answers to questions about things that likely only his grandfather would be able, or willing, to provide. Jacob was now in his thirties and felt it was time for someone to 'own up' and enlighten him. He was perplexed about his childhood and all that had occurred in his family. Jacob had five sisters, all older than him. There was a lot of animosity and distrust from four of his sisters, which he never really understood. He was only close his youngest sister, Jennifer, who was only two years older than him. There was also the matter of his discipline that had grown into a clash between Jacob and his stepmother Vicki. This created an issue in his father's marriage and ultimately resulted in Jacob living with his grandparents when he reached his early teens, just to keep the peace. Now, at this point in his life, a lot of years had passed, and a lot of water had passed under the bridge and he still did not communicate with any of his family, except for Jennifer and, occasionally, his father. It was all very perplexing.

The words from President Upton, when they had 'the talk', continued to resonate in Jacob's head about how his grandfather's and father's way of spreading the Word were unorthodox. What they did seemed normal to Jacob because it was what he grew up with. Now that he was older and other people were pointing out the differences, he was mystified why they both had left the traditional pulpit preaching in a church to go in the directions they had chosen.

As far back as Jacob could remember, early every spring his grandparents would assemble a ragtag troupe of musicians and singers and whip them into a well-tuned musical extravaganza. Grandma Sarah was the musical director but acted more like a Marine Drill Sergeant while forming them into a tight-knitted ensemble. Once ready, everyone would pile into trucks, cars, RVs, campers and a logoed tour bus and go on the road traveling throughout many of the southeastern states as 'Reverend Eli's Traveling Gospel Show'. They put on six shows a week and were seldom in any location more than one day at a time. Each week of the tour, the group would get one day off or their 'Sabbath' as Grandpa Eli would call it. Sabbath was usually spent making repairs to vehicles and equipment, so there was little rest for all involved for weeks on end. Jacob traveled with them when he was living with his grandparents and was always mesmerized by the musicians and choir. While they were on stage performing, and while Grandpa Eli was preaching the virtues of avoiding alcohol and gambling, they were the most professional and pious group you could ask for. However, once the shows ended, and on their days off, they would turn into the least virtuous group of people you ever met. Jacob would sneak around the campers and tents in the evenings and watch them drinking, swearing, gambling, and smoking. He suspected some of their cigarettes were a little more than tobacco, as they smelled a little weird. He often wondered if his grandparents were not aware of the activities or if they just overlooked them.

When Jacob was born, his father was a minister at a very large and growing non-denominational church in Birmingham, Alabama. Jacob was too young to have any recollection of those times. His mother died shortly after his birth and by the time he had reached an age when he could recall any past, the family was living in Nashville where his father wrote and produced Christian music in both the rock and country genres. The only time Jacob attended any formal church services was when one of his father's new songs or a new Christian music group was being debuted to the public, which often occurred at one of the churches around Nashville. While the family did not attend church on a regular basis, his father made sure that everyone was well versed in the Bible with his daily lessons after the evening meal. As a result, Jacob and all of his sisters ended up in the ministry in one way or another. His oldest two sisters became full-time ministers and his other three sisters married ministers. So, with Jacob teaching at a Christian University, his father was batting one-hundred percent in having an effect on his children. As Jacob was driving along, a thought occurred to him . . . with all the turmoil in their home, how could Christianity become so prevalent, and why in the world was he even teaching anything about the Bible when he wasn't sure he even believed in God?

Jacob was suddenly jarred back to the moment when a he saw a car in his lane heading directly toward him attempting to pass another vehicle. Jacob slowed down and pulled off the edge of the road just in time to avoid a head-on collision with somebody who was obviously in too big of a hurry. He decided that maybe he should quit daydreaming and pay attention to the road.

A brief time later he came upon a familiar little town which he had considered as his lunchtime stopping point on the trip. On the far side of town, he came to a little drive-in restaurant that he remembered having good food, hoping it was still in business. The establishment was an old ice cream stand that was likely built back in the nineteen fifties. It was a small building that had two serving windows in the front; the sign on top was the length of the building with faded swirled ice cream cones on each end and the name "Twin Kiss" in the middle. At some point there had been neon lights which had long since burnt out. Sometimes when he and his grandfather were on one of their long drives, Eli would stop there and get a Coney dog. When they were finished, Eli would wink at Jacob and remind him not to tell Grandma Sarah where they had been.

As he pulled into the driveway, he noticed a car parked behind the building and figured someone was there preparing food. Jacob parked in front of the establishment, uncoiled himself from the driver's seat of the Austin Healey and stretched to get feeling back in his extremities. Walking up to one of the serving windows, he was immediately greeted by a smiling young lady who raised the screen and inquired, "Hi sir, what can I get ya?"

Jacob looked at the sign between the serving windows which posted the menu that had several missing letters. "Do you still make that incredible Coney dog?"

"You bet. Would you like me to make you one?"

"Yes ma'am."

"Coming right up sir. Would you like anything else with that?"

Jacob thought about it for a moment considering that he might want to add some French fries, then remembered his recent lunch fiasco and had an image in his mind of how D'Angelo had inhaled all that greasy food. Deciding the 'dog' was going to be far more than he should even consider eating, he replied. "No, that's all, but I will take a diet soda."

"I will have it ready in a jiffy sir. Would you like your drink now?"

"Sure, thank you."

The girl disappeared for a moment and quickly returned with his drink, shoving it through the serving window. "That'll be six dollars and fifty cents sir. I'll have your Coney in a few minutes. I just opened, and things are heating up."

Jacob nodded his acknowledgement and paid the tab. He then took a seat at one of the picnic tables sitting along the side of the building, pulling his cell phone out of his shirt pocket. Jacob had resisted even having a cell phone, but Rebecca insisted that he have one when he traveled so he could stay in touch with her. Not being sure there was even cell coverage where he was at, he typed out a text message letting Rebecca know where he was and sent it. No sooner than he had done that, the girl walked up to his table with his food. "Here you go sir. You are the only one here, so I decided to bring it out to you." The smiling girl then took a seat on the opposite side of the picnic table.

"Thank you. You didn't have to do that." Jacob opened the wrapper around the dog on a bun which was piled high with Coney sauce and onions. Amazed at the size of the thing, he was thinking he might regret this later.

"It's okay. It gets kinda lonely around here until early in the afternoon when the other help gets here. Wow . . . that's a rad lookin' car . . . what is it? I don't think I've ever seen one of those."

The girl had asked the question just as Jacob had taken a big bite out of the Coney; it took a few moments for him to chew, swallow, and wipe his mouth with a napkin before he could answer. "It's an Austin Healey. It's a British car and it's a lot older than you are."

"That's so cool! This is a beautiful day to be driving a convertible. Where are you traveling to?"

"Somerset. My grandfather lives there. I am going to visit him."

"Where are you comin' from?"

"You probably haven't heard of it. Woodlock, Tennessee."

Suddenly a huge grin came across her face, "Woodlock? Of course, I've heard of it. My Granddaddy is some kinda bigwig at Woodlock University. I go there to visit him and my Nana quite often.

Jacob suddenly felt a twinge of uncertainty, half afraid to ask who her Granddaddy might be. "Uh . . . what is your grandfather's name? I probably know him."

"I'm sure you do. His name is Michael Upton."

Jacob gulped hard and had to take a drink of his soda to clear his throat. "Your grandfather is President Upton?"

"Yeah . . . small world isn't it? Next time you see him, tell him his granddaughter Sheila says hi." About then a car pulled into the drive. "Sorry, I gotta go. Have a safe trip to Somerset. You're only about an hour away now." Then she got up from the picnic table and ran around to the back of the building.

Jacob thought to himself, "Small world indeed. What are the chances of running into President Upton's granddaughter this far away from Woodlock?"

Finishing his Coney dog, Jacob picked up his trash and threw it in the container next to the picnic tables and made his way to the car, waving at the girl behind the serving window. She was suddenly going to be very busy as more cars had pulled into the drive, but she wasn't too busy to yell out, "I didn't get your name sir."

"It's Jacob . . . Jacob Prophitt."

"Thanks again Jacob. Have a safe trip. I'll tell my Granddaddy I met you."

Jacob waved again and then crawled into the Austin Healey to get back on the road to Somerset. Pulling out onto the highway, he glanced at his watch and noticed he was making good time and would be at Eli's earlier than expected. From then on, Jacob was driving through familiar territory, making note of the changes that had occurred since he had last been in the area . . . an occasional new home or a building that was no longer there; however, other than that it was mostly the same. Passing along the northern outskirts of Somerset and traveling another few miles past the city, Jacob turned onto a country lane. He passed a couple of homes, which were set deep in the surrounding forest, before coming to Eli's. Jacob pulled into the long, winding, narrow gravel drive that led up to the house, which was lined with a thick growth of trees that blocked the view of the house from the road. When he came to the clearing where the house sat, he immediately noticed his grandfather sitting on the swing on the front porch of the house. Jacob fondly remembered sitting on that swing in the evenings with his grandparents, listening to the birds and the noise of other wildlife in the woods surrounding the house and talking about anything that came to mind.

Before climbing out of the car, Jacob made a quick scan of the house and surrounding yard noticing that things were looking tired and unkempt, unlike the pristine condition it always was when his grandmother was alive. Reaching into his shirt pocket, he pulled out his cell phone and sent a text to Rebecca letting her know he had arrived, again not being sure she would even receive his message. When he opened the car door and began crawling out of Lizzy, his grandfather stood up from the swing and made his way over to the steps on the porch, standing there leaning against a railing post.

Eli Prophitt was built much like Jacob, but not quite as tall. His full head of gray hair was cropped short, which was shocking to Jacob since as far back as he could remember Eli had always worn it long and combed straight back, held down with Brylcreem. He looked much younger than a man in his late eighties, but Jacob noticed that Eli was beginning to get a little stooped over in his shoulders. Other than that, he still looked pretty fit.

"I recognize Lizzy, but I'm not sure I recognize the long-haired, bearded hippy that is getting out of her." Then a wry smile brightened Eli's face as he made his way down the porch steps to meet his grandson. "What's that stuff growing on your chin Son? Can't the famous author, grandson of mine, afford a razor or a decent haircut?" Eli walked up to Jacob and touched the hair on his chin and then patted his cheek like he was giving him a light slap. "Oh well . . . your Daddy went through a hippy stage and he got over it. I guess you could do the same someday."

THE WORDS OF A PROPHITT

Jacob grabbed his grandfather and gave him a big hug and a peck on the cheek, whispering in his ear, "Gee Grandpa, it's really nice to see you too. When you have six hungry kids like I do, you have to cut corners somewhere." He then broke his embrace still holding Eli by the shoulders, "What happened to all your hair?"

"At my age, you need to save all the time you can. Now when I get out of the shower, all I do is dry it off with a towel and I'm done. I figure that's worth ten minutes a day. That all adds up over time." Both Eli and Jacob started laughing and then had another quick hug before Eli broke away with his attention turning to Lizzy. "Well . . . the old girl is looking pretty dapper. You have her shining like a silver dollar. Is she still running good?"

Jacob answered back using one of his grandfather's beloved adages, "Like a sewing machine Grandpa."

Eli walked around Lizzy, carefully caressing her with his hand and inspecting every inch of her. After a long silence he stepped back from the car to give her another once over. "I kind of miss having ole Lizzy around. Oh . . . well, it's been so long since I've driven a stick-shift I probably wouldn't be able to drive her anyway."

"You can have her back Grandpa . . . if you like. I wouldn't mind."

"No Son . . . that would be ridiculous, she's yours now. You're doing a wonderful job of taking care of the old girl. Let's keep it that way." Eli got a faraway look in his eyes as he continued to look over the car; Jacob was hesitant to interfere with his thoughts. Eli, suddenly, started striding toward the house. "I'm glad you made it early. I was just getting ready to hike up to 'the point'. Want to join me?"

Jacob stood motionless, barely able to respond, as he was astonished that Eli was still making the trek up to 'the point' at eighty-eight years of age. 'The point' was a place high upon a ridge on the back side of Eli's property and it was a challenging climb even for a young person. When Eli and Sarah purchased the property, Eli had blazed a path up the ridge and cleared a large area overlooking Lake Cumberland, placing a park bench there. That became their favorite place to go to pray and contemplate life while watching the eagles soar.

Eli returned to the porch and picked up his walking stick. Jacob smiled when he saw his grandfather come down the porch steps grasping it in his hand. It was made from a long oak tree limb with a grape vine coiled around it that Jacob had found while playing on the ridge when he was a youngster. He had fond memories of working with his grandfather, painstakingly peeling off the bark and then watching Eli polish it to a high gloss, creating a beautiful piece of woodwork. Jacob noticed that the stick was getting worn down where Eli had been grasping it while hiking in the woods over the many years. He was then shaken out of his contemplation when Eli yelled out while walking around the house to the pathway up to 'the point', "Hey! Are you coming or not? There's only so much daylight you know!"

"Uh . . . yeah! I'm right behind you!" Jacob had to trot up behind Eli to catch up with him as he was already hiking at a fast pace on the well-beaten path up the ridge. "I can't believe you still hike up to 'the point'."

"I do it every day . . . weather permitting. It keeps me young. By the way . . . keep an eye and ear out for Beauregard."

"Beauregard? Who is Beauregard?"

"Oh, he's just a big ole' timber rattler that decided to take up residency here on the ridge a few years ago."

"Grandpa! What in the heck are you doing hiking out here with a rattle snake lurking around?"

"Don't worry about it. He lets me know when I'm getting too close and I just back off till he moves on and then we're fine. I think we understand each other and respect our territories. Besides, it's my land, he's just a visitor."

Jacob, let out a little laugh, "As I recall from my French class in high school, Beauregard is a name meaning something beautiful . . . how can you call a snake beautiful?"

"Well . . . Jacob, my curious grandson, I just thought it was a proper southern name for the guy, and besides he is beautiful; he's one of God's creatures."

Jacob smiled and continued to follow Eli up the hill, not saying a word to each other, at a pace that would tire a younger man. At the top of the ridge they came to a clearing known to all in the family as 'the point', which provided an inspiring view of God's handiwork. Everyone in the family was taught at an early age that not a soul, except for Grandma Sarah, was allowed into Eli's private sanctuary on 'the point' until the prayer was over, and then they were invited to enter. Jacob, following protocol, stopped at the edge of the clearing as Eli quietly walked over to the edge of the ridge which dropped off to the lake. Eli fell to his knees on a strategically placed log that created a sort of altar, held his arms out wide with his palms up, faced toward the sky with his eyes closed, and began his talk with God.

CHAPTER SEVEN

AFTER WHAT SEEMED LIKE AN eternity to Jacob, Eli Prophitt uttered his 'amen' and arose from the log, walked over to the bench, sat down and remained silent as he stared out at the lake. After a few more moments, with his gaze still fixed, he invited Jacob, "Come join me." Jacob quietly entered the clearing and sat on the bench next to his grandfather. Both remained still, looking out at the scenery. Protocol also required that when one enters the sanctuary, they do not speak until spoken to.

The clearing provided a panoramic view of a northern leg of Lake Cumberland. On most summer days it would be dotted with houseboats and runabouts pulling skiers; however, on this fall day there was only one lonely houseboat traveling on the water below where they sat. Jacob figured it was some late season vacationers getting in their last weekend of boating before the warm weather was over. It was very quiet, other than the sounds of the songbirds and the low hum of the engines on the houseboat. All the stillness and the uncertainty of the anticipated conversation with his grandfather made Jacob a bit uneasy, which made time creep at an incredibly slow pace. Then Eli finally spoke, "I love this time of year. It's not too warm and the leaves are changing, adding color to God's canvas. I like to think of the four seasons as an analogy of life: we are born in the spring and then we reap during the summer." Then came the familiar dramatic pause. "Once we reach autumn, we get to sit back and see the beauty of our lives and enjoy our labors. Finally, we have to face the harshness of winter and the end of life." Eli fell quiet for a few more moments, cleared his throat and continued, "Which is, of course, the precursor to the renewal of life in the spring."

Jacob nodded his head in agreement, not really responding to Eli's comment as he had heard the same analogy from his grandfather many times during his life. Eli often used it during his sermons at his revivals.

"The eagles aren't soaring today. If you look really close you can see their nest across the lake in the top of that dead oak tree."

Jacob scanned the shoreline across the lake and located the tree his grandfather was speaking of. "Yeah . . . I see it."

"I really enjoy watching them soar high above the lake and then take a dive and grab a fish. It just amazes me how they can see a fish in the water from so high in the air."

"Yeah . . . that is amazing."

Then the silence resumed. Jacob could hear his own heartbeat because the atmosphere was so thick with silence. He continued to look up and down the lake, up at the sky, and whatever else he could look at to prevent making eye contact with Eli. Jacob hated it when his grandfather would do that, causing excruciating uneasiness to the person he was about to interrogate, as he would often do to Jacob when he was a kid and was caught doing something he wasn't supposed to be doing.

"I come up here as often as I can to talk with God and your Grandma Sarah."

Jacob, somewhat stunned, turned to Eli, "Do they answer you?"

A tight grin came across Eli's face, still looking straight ahead at the lake. "Well . . . usually not right away, but they eventually do." Then the uncomfortable silence returned, with Jacob being unable to come up with what he thought would be a suitable response. Then Eli finally broke his gaze from the lake and turned to Jacob. "So, Grandson of mine, what's on your mind?"

There it was . . . the door opener. The beginning of the conversation that Jacob desperately wanted to have but was reluctant to begin. Having gone over this moment in his mind several times on how to begin the discussion, Jacob opened his mouth and what came out was, "Not much Grandpa. I just wanted to come and visit with you and see how you are doing." Then his heart sank, feeling like he had just chickened out.

"I see . . . you just traveled a lot of miles to check up on your old Grandpa when we can talk on the phone anytime we like?"

Jacob's heart sank even further, still unable to speak what was on his mind. "Yeah . . . that's pretty much it in a nutshell." Jacob turned back to the lake as if to be searching the sky for the eagles, knowing his face was turning red from embarrassment, something that always happened when he wasn't telling his grandfather the truth.

"Jacob you're blushing. When you blush, you aren't being truthful with me. What's on your mind? Don't be afraid to talk to me son, just speak your piece. You drove a long way. Make it worth your while."

Jacob sat silently, still staring out at the lake trying to work up the nerve to say what he wanted to say. He was full of anger and questions, but his grandfather, even though he was a very gentle soul, was a strong disciplinarian and always an intimidating figure. Then, out of nowhere, a surge of courage hit Jacob and he jumped up from the bench and walked over to the edge of the drop-off to the lake and then spun around facing Eli yelling, "DAMMIT GRANDPA! WHY IS OUR FAMILY SO DISFUNCTIOINAL? WHY DO MY SISTERS HATE ME? HOW DID WE GROW SO FAR APART?" Abruptly Jacob stopped, took a deep breath and lowered his voice, "What about my real mother . . . I don't know anything about her? Why did you and Dad leave the church if you are such strong believers in God? If there really is a God, why does he hate me?"

When Jacob had finished his rant, he stood silently at the edge of the clearing for a few more moments, regretting his outburst. He returned to the bench sitting next to Eli, placed his face in his hands and began sobbing. Eli reached over and began caressing Jacob's back, just like he did when Jacob was upset as a child. After a few moments of silence, Eli spoke, "It's a good thing you packed a bag. It sounds like we have a lot to talk about."

Jacob sat up with tears still rolling down his cheeks. "Grandpa, I'm sorry I blew up like that."

"Don't worry son. Sometimes you just have to let go when you feel like you are carrying the weight of the world on your shoulders. It sounds like you are. I can also tell that you are still mad at God."

"Yeah . . . if there truly is a God!"

Eli straightened his back and returned to gaze out at the lake. "So how is my great-grandson?"

Jacob, now regaining his composure, replied, "He has good days and bad days. Lately with all the fall pollen, it's been a little tough on him but he's doing okay. Unfortunately, the reality is he will probably not make it very far into his teens. The doctors are already discussing a lung transplant; it just kills me to think about it." The tears started welling up in Jacobs's eyes again as he wailed seemingly loud enough so the entire world and the heavens could hear, "IT'S JUST NOT FAIR!" Jacob returned his face to his hands and began sobbing even harder.

Eli returned to caressing Jacob's back, remaining quiet so his grandson could grieve. After a few minutes, he responded, "You know, Jacob, it's okay to be mad at God; all of us have been at one time or another. Heck . . . even King David got mad at God . . . you know what he wrote in Psalms with the Lamentations. I just believe that you need to quit being mad at God and ask for a miracle from Him. He does perform miracles you know. With the incredible strides medical science is making today with so many diseases, who knows . . . they just might eradicate Ezekiel's affliction in his lifetime. You just have to have faith."

The conversation ended there; silence resumed, and Jacob continued to hold his face in his hands while Eli sat back on the bench and returned to scanning the lake. The houseboat that had passed by had stopped farther down from the clearing. The people on the boat had begun swimming and floating around on rafts; the sounds of their conversations and laughter were rising to where Eli and Jacob were sitting, interrupting the quiet. Eli released a huge sigh, "I've had a lot of time to sit and contemplate since your Grandma Sarah passed, and I believe I have come to a conclusion on what has caused this."

Jacob continued sitting with his face in his hands a little longer and then sat up looking at Eli. "I don't understand . . . what do you mean by 'this'?"

THE WORDS OF A PROPHITT

"This . . . the problem we Prophitt men have. The 'this' that you are asking questions about. The 'this' that is the root of all our family issues. It all began a long time ago."

"Grandpa, I'm not following. It's like you are talking in circles."

Eli turned to Jacob. "Son, we Prophitt men are the problem. We are all born with this inherent desire . . . no, strike that. Desire is not the right word. We all have this inbred obsession to have a son to carry on the Prophitt name and it has been the curse of our families."

Jacob was now looking intently at Eli. "Grandpa, I'm still not following."

"This all goes back way before me. You must look at our family tree and it all becomes apparent. It goes all the way back to my daddy and his daddy before him, and his daddy before him and so on. We all have had six children. There have always been five daughters before we have finally had a son, and thus we Prophitt men have had failures in our family relationships. Once we receive a son, we ignore the blessings that God had given us before a son was born. Jacob, your family is young enough that you can avoid the pitfalls of the Prophitt curse."

"So, having a son is a curse?"

"No . . . having a son is a blessing, but so are all of the daughters that came before the son. I made the same mistake my daddy did, and your father made the same mistake I did. You can end 'this' here and now."

Jacob turned his attention back to the lake pondering what Eli had just said. "Grandpa . . . I'm still confused. With all this discussion about curses and blessings . . . I'm not sure who's on first."

"Alright . . . let me spell it out for you. My daddy was a hard-nosed disciplinarian; that was until I came into the world. When I was born, I was the apple of his eye. I got to go everywhere he went, do everything he did and I got to do just about anything I wanted. My sisters, on the other hand, still had to live under his strong-handed ways. All of them were unable to do anything outside of the house without his approval, which was almost impossible to come by. My mother tried to get him to realize what he was doing, but he just ignored her pleas. Thus, all my sisters resented me and they grew to hate Daddy. Each of them couldn't wait until they could leave the house and go out on their own. It was so bad that not one of them attended his funeral when he passed. After Daddy was gone, my sisters all sort of made up with me; however, we were more like casual acquaintances than family. There wasn't a whole lot of love there. Now they are all gone, so what was will always be." Eli stopped talking for a moment trying to gather his thoughts and emotions. Jacob could see tears welling up in his eyes. Then Eli took a deep breath and continued. "I was determined to not be like my daddy, and I did pretty well until your dad was born. Just like my daddy, David became the apple of my eye. Your Grandma Sarah constantly reminded me about what my daddy did, and it helped a little, but I was probably still too hard on all your aunts. All our children traveled with the gospel show and, over time, they all performed in the show. I kept a constant watch over all my daughters, being careful to keep them segregated from all the band and choir members as much as I could. However, I wasn't as vigilant with David. He would often sneak away and hang out with the musicians. I think because of that he grew to become quite the musician himself, able to play all types of instruments. He also learned things that he would have been better off not knowing. As he reached his late teens, he started hanging out with people I didn't care for, but they were all musicians and they all had something in common. He was doing things I wasn't proud of and he was a handful at times. Things had gotten so far out of hand that there wasn't anything I could do to stop it. Finally, when he reached legal age, he announced that he wasn't going to travel with the gospel show anymore and was going to play with a band that he and his friends had formed. He left the show; nevertheless, his sisters were still traveling and performing with us. That just added to their resentment of both me and your father because I let it happen.

Eli stopped talking and Jacob waited for him to continue. Deciding that he wasn't going to finish his thought, Jacob turned to Eli. "Okay I understand all of that and how it could create some animosity, but I don't recall Daddy playing a lot of favoritism toward me. It seems like all we did was argue."

Eli released a loud "HAH", which stunned Jacob. "Jacob . . . the reason you two argued is that you were a snot-nosed, know-it-all brat that always had to get his way! Your daddy and your step-mother couldn't control you. I had to move you here and threaten you within an inch of your life to get you to straighten up. Your daddy loves you whether you want to acknowledge that or not."

Jacob let out a nervous little chuckle. "I guess I should thank you for taking me in and putting me on the right track. I guess I was a handful."

Eli reached over putting his hand on Jacob's shoulder. "It was our pleasure son. We're all proud of what you have become, including your daddy and your step-mother." Eli removed his hand from Jacob's shoulder and sat back on the bench again facing the lake. "Anyway, getting back to your relationship with your sisters . . . your situation is different. There were other circumstances involved."

Jacob waited for Eli to continue, but he didn't. "What do you mean other circumstances?"

"Well . . . your mother died shortly after you were born."

"Yeah, I know that. So, you're saying they hate me because of that?"

Eli paused and took in a deep breath, and then exhaling loudly like he was trying to muster up the courage to continue, "What you probably don't know is what all had occurred prior to you being born."

"Uh . . . yeah, discussions about my mom seemed to be pretty taboo in this family. I really don't know much about her and no one has been willing to tell me anything about her, including my father."

Eli slowly got up from the bench, walked over to the edge of the clearing and peered out over the lake. He stood motionless for several moments and then suddenly spoke while his back was to Jacob. "Your father, to this day, still carries a lot of guilt about what happened. Your mother Roseanne, we called her Rosie, was the most spiritual person I ever met in my life. She was a beautiful lady, inside and out, and she loved everyone, especially her family. She adored your father and was determined to fill his desire to have a son, no matter how many times it took to have one. Well . . . when your youngest sister Jennifer was born, there were some complications that affected your mother physically. The doctors warned your father and mother against having another child because it would be dangerous for her." Eli turned around and returned to the bench next to Jacob. "After much debate, prayer, and soul-searching, David had a vasectomy against your mother's wishes. She was really upset with him for a while after that. Then, lo and behold, as sometimes happens, the procedure didn't take. Your mother got pregnant again. Your father and the doctors did everything they could to try to convince her to abort you, but she said it must have been God's will to have you and she was going to have you no matter what anyone said."

Jacob was starting to get a sinking feeling in his heart, knowing what was coming next. "Wow Grandpa! That must have had everyone on edge waiting for me to be born."

Eli nodded his head in agreement, then turned to Jacob with a smile on his face, "Yeah, everyone but Rosie. She always had a smile on her face and not once acted like she was concerned. She was so busy getting ready for you knowing you were going to be a boy. She was so sure that she got all new baby stuff just for a boy, even though she had a closet full of baby items . . . but it was all for girls. It was almost like she had inside information on something."

Jacob got up from the bench and went to the spot where Eli had stood, looking out over the lake. "That almost sounds a little crazy."

"Oh, trust me Jacob . . . there wasn't anything crazy about your mother. She just had the Spirit in her."

Jacob didn't respond. He just stood there not saying a word. Finally, he turned to Eli. "So, go on with the story . . . even though I'm not sure I want to hear the rest of it."

"Well . . . the rest of the story is that it came time for you to come into the world. Your mother went into labor late in the afternoon and everyone met at the hospital in anticipation of your arrival. Everything went well, and you were born around seven o'clock in the evening. After you were born, the nurse came out and announced it was a boy and told all of us we could visit you and Rosie for a short time. We all walked in and she was holding you with your father standing next to the bed. We all talked and laughed as we were all relieved that Rosie had made it through childbirth. We were all intent in watching her embrace you and as she pulled you up to her lips, she whispered something in your ear. As she handed you to David, she announced that your name was to be Jacob. Then she suddenly moaned in excruciating pain and we summoned the nurse. Your mother was hemorrhaging terribly, and they rushed her to surgery. She passed before midnight . . . there wasn't anything they could do."

Jacob had tears welling up in his eyes as he returned to sit next to Eli. The emotions he was feeling were a combination of sadness about his mother's fate and relief to finally know more about his mother. He was deep in thought, mulling over everything that Eli had just told him when he was brought back to the moment as Eli continued, "I have often wondered what she whispered in your ear. It's strange . . . you had a look on your face like you understood what she had said." Eli glanced over at Jacob who had an expression like he had seen a ghost. "What is it Jacob? You look like you're going to pass out."

Jacob turned to Eli with a look of astonishment and his face seemed to pale. He couldn't speak for a moment, then calmly responded, "I'll tell you what she whispered to me. She said 'I love you little one. We will meet again someday'. Those words have been ringing in my head as long as I can remember. That had to be what she said."

As Eli relaxed back on the bench, he released a huge sigh. "So, she knew her time was over."

"So, that's why my sisters hate me . . . they blame me for our mother's death." Jacob jumped up and returned to the edge of the clearing screaming out over the lake, "WHAT IN THE HELL IS GOING ON?"

"Jacob . . . what is going on? What's wrong with you?"

Jacob, flailing his arms, spun around facing Eli. "I'll tell you what's wrong with me Grandpa . . . my world has been falling apart all around me ever since that stupid book has been published. I took a job teaching a subject I'm not sure I believe in because of the obligation I felt toward the University for getting the book published. I have some publisher bugging the heck out of me to talk about my next book. How can I write another book? My first one was a fluke. My son has a death sentence. My sisters hate me and my relationship with my dad sucks. My first day in class was a disaster. I had this crazy guy wearing golf spikes asleep in the corner of my classroom snoring so loud that I virtually had to yell to teach the class. Then he invites me to lunch and tells me he's there to evaluate me for some Cosmos Industries something or other. The guy was wearing floppy bunny slippers in the diner Grandpa! He was loud and obnoxious. He embarrassed me in front of the Dean of Students and pretty much everyone in the diner. The same day I had the craziest conversation I have ever had in my life with the president of the University, and now . . . after all these years . . . you finally tell me about my mother. That is just the icing on the cake.! I just don't know what . . ."

Eli waved his hands back and forth trying to get Jacob's attention. "Hold on one minute. Let's back the truck up a little. Tell me more about this guy that you were talking about."

"What guy?"

"The guy that you said interrupted your class."

"Grandpa there's not much to tell. He acted like a total buffoon."

"So, Jacob . . . did this buffoon have a name?"

"Uh . . . yeah. What difference does that make?"

"Maybe a lot Jacob. What was his name?"

"Uh . . . I don't know. Oh . . .yeah, I remember . . . I called him Mister D'Angelo."

"JACOB . . . DID HE HAVE A FIRST NAME?"

"Grandpa! Calm down! I don't know what you are getting so upset about. His first name was Michael . . . Michael D'Angelo."

Eli quickly propelled himself from the bench and grabbed his walking stick. Making a beeline toward the path to leave the clearing he exclaimed, "Let's get back to the house! We have a lot to go over. If you think learning about your mother is the icing on the cake . . . son, we haven't even broken the eggs to make the batter!"

CHAPTER EIGHT

ELI PROPHITT MOVED AT FULL stride as he descended the path toward the house. Jacob momentarily stood there motionless stunned for several seconds since Eli had left so abruptly. "Grandpa . . . what's the hurry?" Since his grandfather had left him behind in the clearing, Jacob had to break into a trot to catch up with him.

Eli continued to look straight ahead, barreling down the path. "I told you we have a lot to go over and the day is growing short."

"Grandpa . . . what about Beauregard?"

"Beauregard can take care of himself."

They both made it into the yard and went around to the front porch of the house. Eli climbed the steps, placed his walking stick next to the front door and entered the house, still in a big rush. Jacob had to hesitate for a second since Eli had not bothered to hold the door open for him. Entering the house, Jacob had lost sight of his grandfather. "Grandpa . . . where did you go?"

"I'm here in the office." Jacob walked down a short hallway and entered the room that Eli used as his office. Eli was down on his knees getting a metal box out of a cabinet. Once he had removed it, he got up and sat in his chair and motioned for Jacob to have a seat in a chair in front of his desk. Setting the box in front of Jacob, he declared, "This box contains the deed to this property, all of my bank accounts, all of my funeral arrangements and my Last Will and Testament. I had my attorney set you up as the executor of my estate, so everything you will need to take care of, upon my demise, is in here. I want you to take it with you, so you can be prepared to handle everything when the time comes."

"Grandpa, this is all sort of morbid. I don't like talking about this stuff. Why are you doing this now?"

"My goodness Jacob . . . I'm eighty-eight years old! It's a fact of life and the reality is I'm not long for this world, so you need to man up. Besides, when I'm gone, I want to be sure everything is being taken care of and I have a lot of confidence that you will handle things properly." Jacob stared at the box and it appeared that he was afraid to touch it. Eli sat quietly, waiting for some sort of response from his grandson. Deciding that Jacob didn't have anything else to say, Eli arose from his chair and walked around the desk to leave the office. As he was walking out the door, Eli announced, "Let's go up to the attic. I have a lot of stuff to show you. This is going to answer a lot of your questions."

Jacob, still staring at the 'box of death', was oblivious to what Eli had just said and was unaware that his grandfather had left the room. It then dawned on him that he was alone, so he stood up to leave the office. Standing at the foot of the stairs, he could hear Eli walking around on the creaking floors of the second floor, so he made his way up. On the second story, there were four bedrooms. One of the bedrooms had a large bed where his parents would usually sleep when they visited Eli and Sarah. The rest of the bedrooms were like dormitories with bunk beds where all the children slept. Whenever the whole family came at once, the dorms were packed with kids on bunk beds and in sleeping bags. The eldest parents got to use the bedroom with the large bed and the rest of the adults were spread throughout the house using everything from sofas to recliners to sleep on. Grandma and Grandpa had their bedroom on the first floor and that was where they slept no matter what.

Once he made it to the top of the stairs, Jacob noticed that the door at the end of the hallway was open. This was a door which he was only allowed to enter once before in his life, and that was after Grandma Sarah passed. He had helped Grandpa Eli select a proper gown for her burial. All the children of the family were not allowed to enter the 'attic'. This is where Grandma Sarah and Grandpa Eli kept all their precious treasures from their life together. When Jacob was very young, his sisters had convinced him that the 'attic' was haunted and that he would die if he entered there.

"Jacob . . . come on in." Eli spoke in a softer and kinder voice now, apparently having calmed down. Eli was sitting on a crate next to an old leather trunk which he had opened and from which he was pulling out a shoe box. "This is why I left the pulpit and began the gospel show."

Jacob pulled up an old chair to sit close to the trunk. Taking the shoe box from Eli's hands, he slowly opened it to find a box full of old Christmas cards. Confused, he looked up and asked Eli, "What does a bunch of old cards have to do with you leaving the church?" Eli didn't answer. He just nodded his head indicating to Jacob that he wanted him to take a closer look. Jacob sat the box down and picked out one of the envelopes and pulled out the card. His eyes widened once he read it. He looked up at Eli while reaching for another card. Eli just smiled and watched Jacob. Jacob's eyes widened even more after looking at the second card. Looking at Eli in disbelief, he reached for a third envelope. After opening the third card and reading it, Jacob was speechless. Finally, he stuttered, "Uh Grandpa . . . do you know? I mean . . . do you really? Uh . . . how. . . these cards are all signed by Elvis . . . uh . . . Elvis Presley. How in the world did you know Elvis Presley?"

"I prayed for him and his band one night before a show at a county fair near Huntsville, Alabama."

Jacob looked back down at the card in his hand and then at the box of cards. "Grandpa! Do you have any idea what these are worth?"

"I know what they are worth to me. I have no idea what they are worth to somebody else."

Jacob reached into the box and pulled out more cards. "How many cards are there?"

Eli reached up and started rubbing his hand through his cropped hair. "I'm not sure. He started sending them to me around 'fifty-eight' or 'fifty-nine', and he continued to send them up to around nineteen seventy-six. They came every year at Christmas-time, and they were always hand-written by him."

Jacob sat staring at the box, still not sure what he was looking at or hearing from Eli. "So . . . did you ever meet up with him again?"

"No, he became a big star not long after I met him and his band. They didn't perform much around the small venues when he hit the big time."

"Okay Grandpa, you showed me this big secret . . . but what does Elvis have to do with you leaving the pulpit to start a traveling gospel show?"

"Well . . . when I started preaching, I was just a young man. I got set up at a little church outside of Fayetteville, Tennessee. It wasn't much, but it was a start. One thing you must understand about preachers is that they are human; we all have a desire to do our job well. That can mean having more parishioners, a bigger or newer church, more money in the collection plate and so on. But preachers always have something in their minds that proves to themselves that they are doing an excellent job for their congregations. My gauge to preaching well was that I wanted to be good enough that people would participate in an 'altar call' at the end of my sermon."

Jacob was still leafing through the box of Christmas cards and responded without looking up at Eli, "You mean an altar call where people feel the Spirit, confess their sins and come up to give their life to the Lord?"

"Yes . . . that's what I mean."

Jacob looked up from the box of cards, "Gee Grandpa . . . that's a pretty tall order for saving souls. I don't think that happens very often in the church business. You set yourself up with a pretty lofty goal."

"Yeah, I know . . . but I always set my goals high. That's just a glitch in my character. Anyway, I got out of school and got my first job in that little church. Before I preached on my first Sunday there, so I wouldn't be disappointed, I convinced myself that it would take a while before I got someone to come forward for a blessing, being that I was still a rookie and a little shaky with public speaking. Let me tell you . . . I was scared to death. That church had a lot of old parishioners who had been attending there for many years, listening to the same preacher for most of their lives. The only reason I got the job was that ole Preacher Gibbons passed away suddenly, and they needed someone right then; I got the call because I was next in line at the seminary. Well . . . I got up to the pulpit, preached my heart out, begged and pleaded for the Spirit to overcome the congregation . . . to the point that I was sweating profusely when I was finished. When my sermon was over, I made the request for the altar call and this little elderly lady got up from the back of the sanctuary and made her way up to the altar. My heart jumped, and I was walking on cloud nine."

Jacob had put down the box and was listening intently to Eli. "Wow . . . your first sermon and you got a response to an altar call. That's impressive!"

Eli chuckled, "Not really. You see this went on every Sunday for the next few weeks. I would finish my sermon and then ask for an altar call. Miss Eunice would always come up to get the blessing and no one else would participate. Finally, one of the parishioners informed me that Miss Eunice was suffering from 'hardening of the arteries', which in modern terms is dementia. She could barely remember what she had for breakfast let alone understanding an altar call." Eli started laughing and continued, "So you see, I hadn't really accomplished anything. Miss Eunice would have come to the altar for a chocolate chip cookie."

Both Eli and Jacob had a hearty laugh over Eli's story. Eli again reached into the trunk and pulled out a box with pictures. He chose a few of them, and after sifting through them, he selected one and handed it to Jacob. After taking a quick glance, Jacob exclaimed, "Wow . . . this is you with Elvis and his band! Where was this?"

"That was at the county fair near Huntsville, Alabama."

Jacob was again staring at the photo. "How did that happen?"

Eli continued looking at some more of the photos that were in the box. "I had been having trouble coming up with ideas for sermons. Every Sunday I was standing at the pulpit talking to a bunch of parishioners that were only there because they thought it was an obligation to attend church. I would look out over the sanctuary and see everyone either nodding off or gawking around the room, not really paying attention to what I was saying. So, I was looking for material to shake things up. During that time, that new-fangled music which they were calling 'Rock-a-Billy' or 'Rock 'N Roll' was just becoming popular. I had heard other preachers talking about how sinful it must be by the way kids were reacting to it . . . you know . . . the new dances and things that were happening. A lot of people were convinced it was causing kids to get all worked up and causing them to have sexual relations. So, I decided to do a sermon telling my parishioners to avoid listening to that kind of music because it would cause them to sin. So, I sat down and wrote this scathing sermon that talked about all the terrible things that Rock 'N Roll was causing with our youth. I practiced and practiced that piece until I was blue in the face. When Sunday came, I got up to the pulpit and I yelled and screamed and pounded the pulpit, keeping everyone in church awake. I was getting 'amens' and 'yes sirs' unlike I had gotten the whole time I preached there. The adults were paying attention and the kids were squirming in the pews. I tell you . . . I was on a roll and it felt good. When I got done, my shirt was soaked with sweat and I was exhausted. After that it was time for the alter call . . ." Then Eli stopped speaking and stared off into space like he had lost his train of thought.

Jacob started getting impatient after a few moments and with curiosity asked, "So Grandpa . . . what happened next?"

A broad grin appeared on Eli's face. "I'll tell you what happened . . . as usual, Miss Eunice got up and came to the alter, but then there was a young guy that got up and followed her to the front of the sanctuary. I had never seen him before. He was tall and skinny, wearing a white tee shirt, with a pack of Camel cigarettes rolled up in his sleeve, and black denim peg-legged jeans. He had his hair greased back in one of those duck-tail hairdos. He looked like he came right out of a James Dean movie. He didn't say a word . . . just knelt next to Miss Eunice and accepted my blessing. It was all kind of creepy to me; I didn't know what to think. I was a little afraid of the guy because of the way he looked, but he didn't cause any problems. He just took the blessing and then got up and left the church."

Jacob was now intently looking at Eli, waiting for the next words to come out of his grandfather's mouth. Eli, again, was taking a long pause, causing Jacob to prod him to continue. "So . . . did you ever see this guy again?"

"Yes, I did. After everyone had left the church, I finished tidying up the sanctuary and went out a side door to go home. When I was locking the door, I was startled when someone spoke to me saying, 'That was a pretty good sermon Rev, but you need to get your facts straight before you go talkin' bad 'bout things.' I turned around and he was leaning against his car smoking a cigarette. You should have seen that car. It was a long black Lincoln. I think it was a nineteen forty-nine model. It was all decked out with the hotrod stuff the kids were doing back then like fender skirts, side pipes and spinner hubcaps. It shined like a silver dollar. I had never seen a black car that shiny. Anyway, he flicked his cigarette down on the ground and sauntered over to me to shake my hand. I asked him what his name was and he said it was Michael T Angel."

Jacob leaned forward, putting his hands on his knees, staring at Eli with a confused look, "Ah . . . come on! You must be pulling my leg!"

"No, really and truly. . . that's what he said his name was. I asked him what the 'T' stood for and he said it stood for 'The'. He added that his dad had a warped since of humor."

THE WORDS OF A PROPHITT

Jacob was still looking hard at Eli, not believing what he just heard. "So, you are telling me that this guy's name was Michael 'The' Angel? That's too far-fetched for me to believe!"

Eli laughed out loud at his grandson's response and continued, "I'm telling you the truth. That was his name . . . or that was what he claimed. Anyway, he said he wanted me to go on a little trip with him to meet a good friend of his. Your Grandma Sarah had gone to visit her mother, so I didn't have anything else to do on that Sunday. Also, for some reason I just couldn't resist the guy. His appearance should have usually made me uncomfortable, but oddly enough I really trusted him. So, we climbed into the Lincoln and we headed south toward Alabama, which was just a short distance from Fayetteville. About an hour later, he pulled into this fairground outside of Huntsville where the county fair was going on. We walked around the fair for a while and then we ended up at this stage where acts performed. Michael took me around behind the stage and there he was . . . Elvis Presley. This was about the time that he was gaining popularity with the kids, so he was becoming a real draw for venues like the fair. I had heard a little about him and it was mostly bad; however, most of that information came from adults who were suspicious of his music. When Elvis saw Michael, his eyes lit up as he hurried over to him. As they gave each other a hug, Elvis nearly shouted, 'Michael T Angel, it's so good to see you again! Thanks for stopping by.' Then Michael said to Elvis, 'I want you to meet a friend of mine. This is Reverend Eli Prophitt. I wanted to bring him by to see you perform.' As I reached out to shake Elvis' hand, he grabbed my hand with both of his in a strong grip. 'Reverend Prophitt, it's a pleasure meetin' y'all. Any friend of Michael's is a friend of mine! Come sit down. Let's chat for a spell. We don't go on for another couple of hours." So, we sat and chatted. He was a very nice and very humble gentleman. I could tell that all of the bad stuff I was hearing about him couldn't have been further from the truth."

By now, Jacob was digging through the box of Christmas cards while listening to Eli. Deciding he had seen all he needed, he placed the box back in the trunk. "Wow . . . you met the king of Rock 'N Roll before he was King! But I still don't understand what this all had to do with you leaving the pulpit."

"I'm getting to that Jacob. So, we conversed until it was time for him to go on stage. I was getting up to leave when Elvis had a request. 'Reverend Prophitt, would you do me and the band the honor of leading us in prayer before we go on stage?' I was stunned! Here was this kid playing this so-called evil music wanting me to pray for them. So, I did just that. When I was finished, Elvis and his band went on stage and began performing. Michael took me out front to watch them play their music. I was just flabbergasted at the spell Elvis held over the crowd . . . especially the girls. The audience reacted to his every word and move. It was spellbinding . . . and I didn't really know what to think about what was happening right before my eyes. Michael just smiled at my reaction and chided me, 'See Rev, this stuff isn't evil . . . it's pleasin' to the soul Man! This stuff was created by God. You can't preach against this stuff. You should be usin' it . . . not fightin' it.' Before the show was over, Michael said he had to get on the road, so we headed back to Fayetteville. It was a quiet ride . . . I don't think we said a word to each other the entire trip back home. I was thinking about what I had just seen and heard. When we got back to the church, I shook his hand and got out of the car. I told Michael he was welcome to come back and visit anytime. With a big smile, he told me

'Rev I guarantee we'll meet again someday.' Then he roared off into the night, and I never saw him again."

Eli arose from his seat and reached down into the trunk, digging for another box. After poking around for a few minutes, he pulled out another shoe box. "Here it is. So anyway, what I experienced seeing Elvis perform really weighed on my mind. Every Sunday I was still getting up before a bunch of half-asleep people that weren't listening to a word I was saying. Then it dawned on me . . . I needed to get their attention. And what better way to get people's attention than with music that moves the soul? Your Grandma Sarah was musically talented, so I asked her to put together a little music group and find some lively gospel music and try it out on the congregation. While she was doing that, I wrote some sermons that had a little less fire and brimstone and a little more humor. The first Sunday we tried it out on the congregation, it was a whole new story. The parishioners were clapping to the music with smiles on their faces and then they acted like they were really listening to what I was saying. It was refreshing! After a while, we started taking our little 'show' around to other churches, doing revivals for them. It kept growing more every year and I finally had to quit preaching at a church and went on the road as a full-time ministry. And you know what? When I would make the altar call at the end of our 'shows', I always had people come forward to receive the blessings. Sometimes it would take me an hour to get around to everyone. I felt like I was bringing people to God. There, Jacob . . . that's the story about how meeting Elvis caused 'Reverend Eli's Traveling Gospel Show' to come about."

Jacob looked again at the photo of Eli and Elvis. "Why isn't this Michael guy in this . . . did he take the picture?"

"Uh . . . no . . . it was taken by a photographer. Michael was standing next to Elvis . . . but he didn't show up in the picture." No sooner than Eli had replied, the doorbell rang downstairs. "That must be Misses Kelly from next door with our supper. Grab that box that has your father's name on the top and I'll tell you more about your mom and dad while we eat."

Eli quickly got up and left the room while Jacob was still trying to get his words out. "Uh Grandpa . . . what do you mean he didn't show up in the picture? GRANDPA!"

CHAPTER NINE

Jacob heard voices and laughter coming from the kitchen as he descended the stairway to the main floor. He walked through the dining room into the kitchen to find Eli conversing with a lady who appeared to be in her mid-fifties. Eli saw Jacob enter the room and remarked, "Jacob, I would like you to meet Misses Kelly from down the road. I told her you were coming to visit and she insisted on making us her special lasagna for our dinner. She and her husband make it a point of being nosy about what I am doing to make sure I'm alright." Eli glanced over at Misses Kelly with a sly grin on his face and winked at her. "I tell you, it gets very annoying."

Jacob approached Misses Kelly, holding his hand out for a handshake. "It's a pleasure to meet you Misses Kelly. I'm Jacob Prophitt." Misses Kelly would have nothing to do with a handshake, but rather grabbed Jacob and proceeded to give him a big hug as Jacob looked over her shoulder at Eli with a stunned look.

She then released her hug and replied, "Oh, please . . . call me Jules. Let's dispense of that Misses Kelly stuff. Believe me, I know who you are. Eli has told me all about the renowned author in his family."

Jacob, feeling a twinge of embarrassment backed away from her and walked around to the opposite side of the kitchen table from where she was standing. "Well, Misses . . . I mean Jules, I appreciate that you are watching over Grandpa."

Jules then walked over and began opening kitchen cabinets. "Eli . . . where are your dinner plates? I need to get this lasagna dished out while it's still warm. Oh, here they are." She began pulling some plates out, setting them on the kitchen counter next to the dish she had brought, "Oh dear it's not a bother. Eli is one of the sweetest people I have ever met . . . and he's been very helpful to us. My husband is not the handiest person in the world and Eli has come over to our place to show him how to fix a few things. Jim and I try to keep an eye on your grandfather as much as we can. It just worries us to death about him making that climb up the ridge as much as he does. A man his age could fall and break a hip or something else and not be found for a long time. And then there's that darn rattlesnake that lives up there . . . what do you call that thing Eli?"

Eli looked at Jacob with a grin on his face. "Beauregard . . . his name is Beauregard."

"Yeah Beauregard. It's just not safe for Eli to be tromping up and down that hill with a darn rattlesnake lurking around . . ."

Eli decided to interrupt to change the subject. "Jules, you need to get out a dish for yourself and join us for dinner."

"Oh, that's not going to happen. Jim is taking me to the VFW for a pitch-in dinner they are having. They are going to have a DJ, so there's gonna be some drinkin' and dancin' goin' on. Oh! Look at the time . . . I must get going. You guys enjoy this lasagna. I put some salad in the fridge . . . bye!" She then spun on her heels and tore out of the house like she was on fire.

THE WORDS OF A PROPHITT

 Jacob and Eli looked at each other at the same time and then started laughing as Eli roared, "She's really something, isn't she?" Eli picked up the filled plates and placed them on the kitchen table as Jacob went to the refrigerator to get the salad.

 "So, Grandpa . . . what did you mean this Michael guy didn't show up in the photo?"

 Eli, avoiding Jacob's question, pulled some drinking glasses out of a cabinet, "What do you want to drink? I have soda pop and tea, or you can have water if you like. I think I'll have water." Then Eli went over to the kitchen sink and filled his glass from the water tap. "I don't know what to tell you Jacob . . . the photographer took down my address and told me he would send me a copy of the picture. When it came, there was no Michael in it. I know he was standing next to Elvis; I was there when the picture was taken. The photographer sent a note with the picture saying he didn't know why the other man wasn't in the photo and that something like that had never happened to him before."

 The two of them then sat down at the table preparing to eat and bowed their heads as Eli began the prayer. Jacob, knowing his grandfather, figured that the lasagna would get cold by the time Eli reached the 'amen'. However, he was surprised when Eli finished in just a few sentences. Eli took a bite of the food on his plate and then reached for the box Jacob had brought down from the attic. Taking the lid off and digging around the pile of photos that were inside, Eli pulled one out and handed it to Jacob. "This is a picture I wanted you to see."

 Jacob took it from his grandfather and looked it over. "So, Grandpa . . . what is this supposed to be? It looks like a bunch of hippies."

Eli looked at Jacob while chewing his food. Once he could swallow what was in his mouth, he replied, "That's exactly what that is . . . a bunch of hippies . . . but the hippies in the middle are your mom and dad."

Jacob had been holding the picture with one hand while eating with the other. He laid his fork down, grasped the picture with both hands, and began examining it closer. "My mother and father were hippies? This is crazy . . . where was this picture taken?"

Eli got up from the table going over to the kitchen counter to get another helping of the lasagna. He stopped while he stared right into the cabinet door, "I can't remember the name of the place. It was some kind of huge rock concert and peace rally back in the late sixties, up in Upstate New York somewhere."

"Grandpa . . . are you talking about Woodstock?"

Eli had loaded his plate and was returning to the table. "Yeah . . . I think that was what it was called . . . yeah, Woodstock."

"You're telling me that my mom and dad went to Woodstock together?"

"No . . . not together . . . they met there. Your dad went to Woodstock with his band buddies. Here, let me show you something." Eli reached back into the box on the table and pulled out another stack of photos. He began pealing them off until he found what he was looking for. "Here it is. This is a picture of your dad and his friends right before they left to go to that concert."

Jacob took the picture from his grandfather and sat back in his chair. He was looking at four guys with long hair and beards, wearing faded jeans with huge bell-bottoms, leaning up against an old Ford station wagon. He began laughing, "Wow! This picture looks like an album cover for a sixties psychedelic band. I can't believe my dad ever looked like that. Does that say 'welcome wagon' on the side of that car?"

"It sure does. That's what they called her; they drove that thing everywhere. One of his friends had a brother that was quite the artist. He airbrushed a bunch of peace signs and flowers all over the car; then he dubbed it the 'welcome wagon' and painted that on the doors. They ended up driving that thing to New York. I begged and pleaded with them not to go, but there was no stopping them, so I pitched in some gas money in hopes that they would get there and back . . . and to be honest, I wasn't sure they planned on coming back."

Jacob laid the picture down on the table and continued eating. "Why were you worried about them coming back?"

"Because this was during the Viet Nam War. These guys were just out of school and at the prime draft age. Your daddy was vehemently against the war. In fact, he was listed as a 'conscientious objector'. The local draft board people were watching him very closely. He always told me that if they tried to draft him, he would go to Canada and expatriate before he would participate in a politically trumped-up conflict that was costing innocent lives. So, I figured if he and his buddies got that close to Canada, they would be gone. And if your daddy hadn't met your mother there, I'm still not sure if he would have come home."

Jacob took another bite of food and while appearing to be, but not really, looking at his grandfather, "How in the world did mom and dad meet at a place like Woodstock? There were over a half-million people there."

"Your daddy told me that when he and his buddies got there, they couldn't get any closer to park than five miles from where the stage was. While they were walking to the concert, they cut across an open field following other people, hoping those people knew where they were going. On the way, they came across a pond where people were bathing and swimming. David said he saw this guy that looked exactly like he envisioned Jesus, with shoulder length hair and a beard, wearing a white robe, and he was baptizing people in the pond. He said he didn't know why, but he was drawn to this guy and had to get closer to see what was going on. His buddies got upset with him because he wanted to stop there, so he told them to go on ahead and that he knew where the car was and would meet them back there if he didn't find them. He went on to say that when he got closer, he saw that the guy was inviting the people who were standing around the shore to come in and get baptized, and that a lot of them were doing so. Your daddy said that he tried to stay behind the crowd so as not to be noticed, but he just couldn't keep his eyes off the guy and what he was doing. He was just about to leave to find his buddies when that guy yelled out 'David . . . come join me in the water'. Your daddy said that everyone started looking around, apparently looking for a David. The crowd in front of him parted like the Red Sea and he found himself standing there right in the sight of this guy; the guy held out his hand, beckoning him into the water. Your daddy told me that his head and heart said to turn and run . . . but his feet took him right into the water . . . clothes and all to get baptized. He said it was the strangest feeling he had ever experienced." Eli slowly arose from the table, picking up his plate and utensils, taking them to the sink; then he returned to his place across the table from Jacob. "I'll do dishes in the morning. Just put your dish in the sink when you are finished."

Jacob laid down the picture of his father and his buddies and picked up the picture that his mother was in, examining it. "My gosh. She was beautiful, even as a hippie. So how did Daddy meet Mom there?"

"I'm getting to that Jacob . . . just be patient. Anyway . . . your daddy got baptized by this guy and then he announced to the crowd that he was done and that he would be back the next day to continue the baptisms if anyone wanted to join him. He then told your daddy that he wanted him to come to his camp and that he had someone there that your daddy should meet."

"So, Grandpa, did this guy have a name?"

"Sure . . . he told your daddy that his full name was Miguel Angelo . . . but he preferred to just be called Angel."

Jacob's face turned flush and then red like he was getting mad. "Oh, c'mon Grandpa . . . what kind of a fool do you take me for? Michael . . . Miguel . . . Angel . . . Angelo . . . they all translate out the same. I didn't travel this far for a tall tale."

Eli placed his elbows on the table, grasped his hands together and lay his chin on them, staring at Jacob, "So Jacob, what did you say the guy's name was that interrupted your classroom?"

"It was . . . well it was . . . uh . . . Michael . . . uh . . . Michael D'Angelo."

"So, Jacob . . . is your story a tall tale?"

Jacob, having been holding the picture of his parents the entire time Eli had been talking, now laid it down on the table, "Uh . . . no Grandpa . . . sorry. Please, go on."

Eli unclasped his hands, sat back in his chair and continued, "Your daddy said he followed this Angel guy back to a campground area, and that there were a lot of people hanging around in the camp. He noticed that there were people serving food, water, and wine to anyone who wandered in and asked to be fed. He also said that supplies were running out at the concert venue since the promoters had underestimated the crowd, but somehow in Angel's camp the supplies seemed endless. Your daddy told me that when he and Angel entered the camp, he noticed a beautiful girl working as one of the servers, and that he immediately fell in love. Angel led your daddy over to her, introduced her as Rose and told them that he believed they belonged together. I don't think your daddy left her side from that moment on, literally."

Jacob reached down and picked up the photo of his mother and father, taking another brief look at it, "So how in the world did my mother end up back at home with dad?"

"That's the crazy part, Jacob . . . you see after a couple of days David's buddies came looking for him and ended up at the camp where your daddy was working with your mom feeding the hungry. It was getting close to the end of the concert and everyone was starting to get ready to head home. Your daddy said that your mom's friends had disappeared and she had no way to get back to where she lived. So, they offered to take her home. When they asked her where she lived, it ended up that she only lived about twenty miles from where we lived in Tennessee."

"Grandpa, that is absolutely unbelievable . . . traveling all the way to Woodstock and meeting up with someone that lived that close to you! That's just incredible!" Jacob scanned over the photo again and then suddenly erupted, "WHOA! I recognize the guy standing next to mom! That's Jimi Hendrix! How in the hell . . ."

"Oh yeah . . . I forgot that part. David said that Angel took him, your mom, and his buddies backstage to meet some of the musicians. He said that it seemed like everyone there knew who Angel was. Your daddy was a big fan of Mister Hendrix; he told me that he was one of the best guitarists that ever lived. David went on to tell me that there was a guy there with one of those polaroid cameras . . . you know . . . the ones that would develop in sixty seconds. Angel

THE WORDS OF A PROPHITT

asked him to take a picture of him and his group with Mister Hendrix. And that's how that picture came about."

Jacob continued to stare at the photo. After a few moments, he looked up at Eli with a puzzled expression. "Wait a minute . . . you say that this Angel guy was with the group? I don't see anyone that looks like Jesus in this photo."

"Uh . . . yeah . . . about that, your daddy said that when the picture was taken, everyone gathered around to watch the photo develop. When it was done, there was no Angel in the photo. He was supposed to be standing next to Mister Hendrix. When they looked for Angel, he had disappeared . . . nowhere to be found. David said that when they returned to the campsite looking for him, the camp was gone . . . like it had never been there at all."

Jacob laid the picture of his parents in the box with the rest of the photos. "Grandpa this is getting way too weird. Nobody could make up a story like this. You have these guys appearing and disappearing into thin air and not appearing in pictures that supposedly they were in. That can't be possible. When did Daddy tell you all this stuff anyway . . . and why not share it with any of us kids?"

"Your daddy came and stayed with me for a few days after your Grandma Sarah passed, to make sure I was okay. We got to spend some time together and we had a few heart-to-heart discussions. That's when he shared all of this with me. He made me swear that I would never tell a soul; however, I feel like someone needs to know the story. It's part of your family history. David has been carrying the weight of the guilt over your mother's death and he can't let go. This is all so painful for him, even today, but I'm getting old and if I don't tell you about it, he might take this to his grave. Then none of you kids would have known how your parents met and the circumstances around your mother's death."

"This does explain something I never understood."

"What's that Jacob?'

"One time my sister Robin and some friends rented a movie about Woodstock. While they were watching it, Daddy walked in the room to see what they were watching. After a few minutes, he got all teary-eyed and left the room, not saying a word." Jacob sat quiet for a moment as if in deep thought. "Alright Grandpa . . . I'm still unconvinced. But for the sake of conversation, what happened next?"

"Well, what happened next is that your daddy and mother came back from the concert and rushed out and got married. Your daddy cut off his beard and his long hair and entered a Christian seminary to become a preacher. Your mother became pregnant with your oldest sister almost immediately, so they came and lived with me and your grandma while he went to school. Your daddy took on odd jobs and taught musical instruments to make the money to live on. During our traveling season, they both worked in the gospel show. Your daddy played in the band and did a lot of the arrangements and your mother sang. Oh Jacob . . . I tell you, she had the voice of an angel. When she sang, people wept. She was that good!" Eli got up from the table and headed toward the door. "Come . . . follow me. I have something for you."

Jacob followed Eli and they ended up back in the office. Jacob felt a nervous twinge as he looked at the 'box of death' still sitting on Eli's desk. Eli pulled another box off a shelf and laid it on the desk. While opening it he commented, "This is a box of CD's that I put together for you and your sisters. Your daddy had taped some of the gospel shows on a reel-to-reel recorder, but the darn thing broke down and I found a guy that could transfer the tapes to CD's to preserve them." Eli then pulled out a few and shuffled through them until he found what he was looking for. He then found a small CD player with headphones in his office desk and handed it to Jacob. "I thought you might like to hear what your mother sounded like. I'm going to bed. It's getting late for me, but you can stay up and listen to this for a while if you like. Eli began to exit the office, then stopped and turned facing Jacob. "I have some things I would like to get done around the place tomorrow if you wouldn't mind helping me out." Jacob smiled and nodded his reassurance to Eli. "Good, I'll see you bright and early. Goodnight. Don't stay up too late."

"Goodnight Grandpa." Jacob sat looking at the CD and player in his hand, reluctant to play the disc, not sure what to expect. After a long pause trying to get up enough courage, he inserted the disc into the player and put on the earphones. Holding the player, it seemed like he didn't have enough strength in his finger to push the play button. Once he did, the first thing in his ears was the sound of Eli making an introduction, talking about the newest member of the gospel choir. Then there were some rattling noises while someone was adjusting the microphone on stage. Then a woman began speaking about how she had found Jesus and had given her life to Him. Jacob's mind suddenly went into overdrive listening to the voice as there was something very haunting about it. He couldn't immediately put his finger on what it was. He continued listening more to the voice than to what the lady was saying when it suddenly struck him, and he uttered out loud, "Oh God . . . that's the voice that's been in my head my whole life!" Jacob shut off the player to regain his composure, hoping he hadn't woken Eli with his outburst. He pulled off the headphones, listening for any movement from his grandfather. Once he was convinced everything was alright, he put them back on and continued playing the disc. He was now listening to what the lady was saying with more interest. Then the voice stopped speaking and began singing "Amazing Grace". Jacob was now certain that the angelic voice that was singing was in fact his mother's. He had never heard the song done so beautifully in his entire life. He had never missed his mother before, having never known her, but now he felt a loneliness he had never experienced before. Suddenly overcome with emotion, Jacob slid off his chair onto his knees and quietly sobbed as the voice of his mother sang to her son.

CHAPTER TEN

JACOB AWOKE TO THE CHIRPING of songbirds outside his window and the familiar aroma of bacon frying. Once he opened his eyes, he realized that the sun had risen and, obviously, Eli was up making breakfast. There was no clock in the bedroom where he had ended up going to sleep, so he wasn't sure how early or late it was. He just knew that if Eli was up and he was supposed to be up also. Rolling out of bed, he grabbed his safari attire and made his way down the hall to the bathroom. While at the sink brushing his teeth, Jacob looked in the mirror and noticed his eyes were still red and puffy, no doubt from crying himself to sleep. By now he felt like he was totally out of tears. He splashed water on his face and eyes, attempting to look normal, and headed downstairs. When Jacob entered the kitchen, Eli looked around with a big smile on his face. "Good morning sunshine. How are you this beautiful Kentucky morning?"

Jacob shuffled over to the coffee maker and poured himself a cup. "I'm fine."

"From the look of your eyes, you don't look fine. Rough night?"

"Yeah . . . it was a little rough, but I'll be okay."

"Still like your eggs over-easy?"

Jacob took a sip of coffee and thought for a moment before answering. Then looking up at Eli answered, "Yes . . . that would be great. I haven't had your fried eggs forever."

Eli let out a little chuckle. "Okay . . . over-easy coming up. Help yourself to the toast, this will be ready in just a couple of minutes."

Jacob sat quietly drinking his coffee while deep in thought, replaying in his mind all the conversations with Eli the day before. His train of thought was interrupted when Eli placed a plate of eggs and bacon on the table in front of him. "Here you go. Are you sure you're alright?"

"I'm fine Grandpa. I just feel a bit overwhelmed with everything we talked about yesterday . . . and then hearing my mother's voice and realizing I've had her voice in my head my whole life. It's all so surreal."

Eli returned to the table with his plate of food and sat down across from Jacob, immediately bowing his head in prayer. Jacob followed suit and remained quiet until his grandfather was finished. When Eli uttered his 'amen', he started digging into his plate of food like he hadn't eaten in days, not saying a word or looking up at Jacob. Feeling uncomfortable with the silence, Jacob spoke, "You know Grandpa . . . I woke up last night and I swear I heard what sounded like a rattlesnake outside my window."

Without looking up at Jacob, Eli replied, "Yeah, that's Beauregard. He comes down from the ridge at night. He is sort of my guard snake; he keeps the critters away from the house."

"Grandpa doesn't it worry you that he's slithering around out there so close to the house?"

With a stern look, Eli looked up at Jacob. "Jacob, I stay inside and he stays outside . . . there is no problem with that."

THE WORDS OF A PROPHITT

Jacob decided that it would be better to drop the subject before he got under his grandfather's skin. After a long silence, and a few bites of food, Jacob continued with another line of questioning. "So, Grandpa . . . last night you were telling me about Daddy becoming a preacher, and I kind of knew about that, but I don't remember ever seeing him preaching in a church."

"That's because he quit the church when you were just a baby."

"Why did he do that?

Eli continued eating without saying a word for a few moments. He then laid down his knife and fork and sat back in his chair looking at Jacob. "I guess after all of the bean-spilling I've been doing since you came, I might as well tell the rest of the story. I will be in trouble anyway if David finds out about this. I'm asking you to keep all of this to yourself until I'm gone . . . agreed?"

"Sure Grandpa, you have my word. You keep talking about when you're gone. I don't think that is something that is going to happen soon."

"Jacob, tomorrow was never promised. Always remember that." Eli got up from his chair, went to the coffee maker, poured another cup and then returned to sit at the table. "So, as you remember, I told you about your daddy coming back and going to school to be a preacher. He and your mother worked on the tour with your Grandma Sarah and me to make extra money while he was in school. When he graduated, with high honors I might add, he immediately got a position as an associate pastor at a large progressive church down in Knoxville. David and your mom became immediate hits there. Everyone at the church just loved Rosie. She was involved in all the women's groups, and your daddy took over the musical arrangements and included some modern

Christian music in some of the services. That church was big to begin with, but then it suddenly began growing by leaps and bounds when word got out about the new style of worship. A lot of younger people started attending with their families and the church started getting cramped for space and they had to build an addition onto the church. After he had been there for three or four years . . . I don't remember how many for sure. . . the head pastor decided to retire and the church council offered the position to your daddy and he accepted it. Well, let me tell you what, that church just exploded! After a couple of years, they had to build a whole new church to accommodate the growth they were experiencing. Your daddy's musical services were becoming legendary and your mom and daddy were riding a tall wave and were on top of the world . . . then you were born."

Eli got up from the table and began picking up the breakfast plates and silverware, putting them in the kitchen sink without saying another word. Jacob was now on the edge of his seat waiting for his grandfather to continue. "Grandpa . . . that's it? I was born and that's the end of the story? Why did Dad quit the church?"

Eli placed both hands on the countertop and gazed out the window over the sink. He remained quiet for a few more moments, then turned to Jacob while leaning back against the counter. "When Roseanna died, everyone in the church was devastated. All the church members rallied around David and helped in any way they could with all of you kids and his emotional well-being. It was very tough for your daddy, especially for the first few months, so he buried himself in his work at the church to avoid having to deal with your mother's death. Well . . . at that time, your step-mother, Miss Vicki, was working as the church secretary. Ironically, Rosie had hired her, a couple of months before you were born, to take over the office duties while your mother was preparing to have you." Eli stood up straight from leaning on the counter, returned to the table and sat down. "David said that your mom told him that Vicki was meant to be there and that she needed the support of the church. She had married her high school sweetheart after he had been drafted and right before he had left for Viet Nam. A short time later, her husband was declared 'missing in action', never to return. She had taken it really hard and was carrying a lot of emotional baggage . . . so much that she had not dated anyone for several years . . . until . . . well . . . you know how misery loves company."

"I'm guessing that's when Daddy started dating Vicki?"

"Yes, and they did their best to keep it quiet. Eventually people started figuring it out and the busy-bodies in the church started making a big deal out of it because they loved your mother so much. They thought it was too soon for your daddy to be dating other women, especially the church secretary. Well, because of that, there was beginning to be a lot of dissention in the congregation and they finally forced the church council to give your daddy an ultimatum. They wanted Vicki fired and he had to stop dating her to continue as head pastor of that church."

"So, that's when Daddy quit preaching?"

"No . . . not exactly. He asked the council for a sabbatical to clear his head and decide what he wanted to do. They agreed and he took some time off. One night he showed up at our doorstep with you kids. He dropped all of you off and said he was going to take a trip and that he would be back in a few days . . . and then he was gone."

"Was Vicki with him?"

"No, he was by himself."

"Where was he going?"

"At the time, David didn't say where he was going... just that he was going. However, years later I found out what happened when he was recounting everything. Your daddy said that he decided to return to Upstate New York to the town of Woodstock, where the concert had been held. He didn't know why, just that he was compelled to go there. He drove the same route that he and his buddies took when they were going to the concert and by now had been driving for a couple of days. When he got within an hour or so of where he was intending to go, he had to pull over and get some rest. He said he came upon an old roadside motel that had a vacancy sign flashing, so he decided to stop and get a room. On his way to his room he noticed a roadhouse next to the motel that was open with a sign in the front window saying they served food. After he took his suitcase to his room, he decided to go there and see what they had to offer. He said that when he walked in the only people there were a couple of guys shooting pool and the bartender, who was sitting behind the bar with his back to David, watching television. When your daddy sat down at the bar, the bartender spoke without even turning around, 'David my old friend... I've been expecting you.' David said he was absolutely stunned when he heard him say that, and when the guy turned around David was shocked that it was Miguel."

"Miguel? You mean the guy they called Angel that Baptized Daddy at Woodstock?"

"The one and only! Your daddy said he almost fell off his barstool when he saw him. He said he still looked like Jesus with his long hair and beard, but he was wearing a baseball cap. David said Miguel walked up to him and sat a glass on the bar in front of him and said, 'You look like a man that could use a tall glass of wine.' Your daddy said he was hesitant to drink it as he had not had any alcohol for several years; however, Miguel was insistent, so he decided it wouldn't hurt to have one drink. He said that Miguel made him a sandwich and continued to fill up his wine glass while they talked through the night. Your daddy said they talked about everything and that Miguel was very compassionate and understanding as well as providing some helpful viewpoints about your daddy's situation. David said that later when the wine started affecting him, he got very sleepy. He woke up in his room the next morning, not sure how he got there and had a terrible wine hangover. After getting cleaned up, he decided to see if he could get some breakfast and coffee at the roadhouse; however, when he walked over to see if they were open, he found that the place was all boarded up. The lady in the motel office told him that the place hadn't been open for business for more than three years."

"Grandpa . . . I think Daddy must have been inebriated way before he got to that roadhouse."

Eli laughed at Jacob's comment and continued. "Well I don't know about that, but David went on to Woodstock, got some breakfast and then took a drive by where the concert was held, and then headed back home. He stopped here for a couple of days to visit and then took you kids back to Knoxville. When he got there, he immediately resigned as pastor of the church, married Miss Vicki, and then packed everyone up and moved to Nashville to start a new career as a songwriter and music producer. That's when your daddy quit preaching."

Jacob leaned back in his chair and started rubbing his face with his hands. He remained quiet for a few seconds and then dropped his hands to look at Eli. "Is there anything else that you need to add to these crazy stories? Did Daddy share anything about what this Miguel guy told him that would make him just jump off a cliff like he did?"

Eli got up from the table and began cleaning up the breakfast dishes. "No . . . he didn't share that with me. Your daddy had a profound change in him after making that trip. However, he certainly hasn't done too bad for himself and you kids' by making the move. He's been quite successful in his new career." Eli finished placing the breakfast dishes in the sink, then turned to Jacob. "I would like for you to help me move some stuff in the barn so I can get to a couple of trailers in there. I sold them and the guy is coming tomorrow to haul them away. I don't think I can do it by myself. It won't take us long and then you can get on the road. We can talk some more while we are working." Eli headed for the door and then turned to Jacob. "And young man . . . do not forget the box on the desk! You are not leaving here without it! Understand?"

Jacob nodded his acknowledgement, got up from the table and made his way down the hall to the office. There it was . . . right in the middle of the desk . . . the 'box of death'. Scared to even touch it, he took a deep breath, then reached out to pick it up . . . then pulled back hesitating . . . then finally put his hands on it and picked it up. Holding it gingerly, he carried it out of the house and placed it in the boot of the Austin Healy, intending to leave it there and ignore it altogether. Hearing some noises coming from the barn, Jacob decided he had better get to work before Eli hurt himself trying to move things around without any help. Walking toward the barn, Jacob thought to himself, "I think Grandpa is getting senile. These crazy stories he's been telling me are too weird to be true."

Once everything was moved around to Eli's satisfaction, Jacob went into the house, packed up, loaded the car, gave his grandfather a hug and then headed east toward Woodlock. The drive from Grandpa Eli's was uneventful, other than the constant rehashing in Jacob's mind about the conversations he had with his grandfather, as well as all the other conversations and occurrences before visiting Eli. While on the road home, Jacob had decided to forgo another Coney dog at the 'Twin Kiss' and to stop for a salad at a roadside diner. He realized that his two-day diet of hot dog, pasta, and eggs and bacon was about all his body could tolerate without having something with roughage in it. So, he returned to his Spartan diet of a salad with an oil and vinegar dressing. Once Jacob returned to the road, he was so engulfed in trying to decipher everything that he drove Lizzy through the mountains like he was an old man on a Sunday drive, creeping along at a snail's pace. The trip home took longer than usual; it was late Sunday night before Jacob finally made it back to his family. When he got home, the only person awake was Rebekah who was waiting up for him to return. All the children had gone to bed early to get ready for school on Monday.

CHAPTER ELEVEN

IT HAD BEEN THREE DAYS since Jacob returned home from Somerset. Things were going reasonably well, other than a short stint in the hospital with Ezekiel, for some antibiotics to fight off an infection which, unfortunately, was occurring more frequently. Jacob was home from his weekly teaching session at the University and had prepared supper for the family since Rebecca had to work a late shift at the hospital. The evening meal was finished and the children were at their typical areas doing homework, so all was quiet at the Prophitt household.

Jacob had retreated outside to the back-porch swing, sipping on a glass of tea, listening to the sounds of nature and attempting to relax while continuing to rehash the conversations with his grandfather for the hundredth time. He was still trying to decide whether all the stories Eli had shared with him were fact or fiction and, more importantly, was there any correlation between Michael D'Angelo, Miquel, and Michael T or were they all just a huge coincidence? Jacob pondered the questions at length. 'D'Angelo was such a buffoon. How could he possibly be connected to the other guys . . . or was it just an act? How did President Upton know D'Angelo? Also, there was the issue with age differences. If D'Angelo was the same guy as the others, he would have to be a lot older . . .

unless he was a . . . no, that's not possible. And how did the other two disappear from the photos? Maybe they were . . . no, that's not possible either. There had to be an explanation . . . or was it all fiction? And what about Grandpa Eli meeting Elvis and the strange disappearance of Miguel after his father's meeting with Jimi Hendrix? How about the irrational story about the roadhouse? If those things had really happened . . . they would have had to have been ghosts or, dare say, angels? If that were true . . . that would mean there was a God . . . no, that's just not realistic . . . or is it?'

Jacob was abruptly brought back to reality when he heard laughter nearby. He looked around the back yard, but nobody was there. He sat his glass down and, with hesitancy, walked over to the railing on the porch and looked up to the clearing on the hill above the backyard. Since it was early dusk, he could only make out the dim glow of what appeared to be a campfire, just like he had seen on several occasions since moving into the house. It was always at early dusk and again he figured it was some students out partying in the evenings. However, this was the first time he had heard any noise from up there. Jacob had ridden his mountain bike to the clearing many times on days when he didn't have class, but he was never able to find any remnants of a campfire . . . or even any sign of anyone having been there. So, he assumed, whoever it was must have been using a camping stove and doing an excellent job of cleaning up after themselves. Deciding to ignore the interruption, Jacob returned to the swing and attempted to get back to his thoughts. After a brief time, the laughter occurred again. Jacob, again, got up and stood at the railing. While staring up at the clearing he heard more laughter and, for some reason, was suddenly overtaken by an overwhelming urge to find out who it was, thinking that he should go reprimand them for being out partying in the woods when it was beginning to get dark. There was a chance they could get caught in the path of a black bear beginning its nighttime foraging for food, which could be very dangerous. Jacob turned and walked to the back door and entered the kitchen where his oldest daughter, Bethany, was sitting at the table working on her assignment. "Honey, I'm going for a quick ride up the hill to check out something. I'll be back in a few. You're in charge until I get back."

"Okay Daddy . . . be careful."

Jacob exited the house and went to the garage to retrieve his mountain bike. Reaching up on a high shelf, he grabbed a helmet that he had rigged up with a flashlight, which made it look like a miner's hat. He often used it when riding at night to see, and to be seen. Jacob put on the helmet, pushed the bike out onto the driveway, mounted it, rode out of the driveway and began peddling down the road. After traveling a short distance, he turned onto an old fire trail that would take him up to the clearing. At first the grade on the trail was gradual but, as Jacob rode further up the hill, the path steepened. This was a ride he had taken on many occasions for a cardio workout, thus he was adept at adjusting the gear ratios on his bike to make the climb easier. After being on the trail for about ten minutes, Jacob arrived at his destination. He peddled into the clearing, dismounted his bike and put down the kickstand. Jacob immediately noticed a woman with bright green eyes, platinum blond hair and an olive complexion sitting in a lawn chair next to a campfire reading a book. She let out a hearty laugh, not paying any attention to Jacob. As Jacob removed his helmet, he interrupted her. "Uh Miss . . . is there something I can help you with?"

The woman in the chair raised her hand, held up one finger while continuing to read. "Give me a moment. I'm just about done with this chapter." She read for a few more moments and then started laughing hysterically. She closed the book and laid it on the ground. Gathering her composure, she looked up at Jacob while still in her chair and continued, "That's the biggest bunch of tripe I have ever read. Doctor Prophitt, you have a great imagination! I can't believe you have theologians clamoring over this stuff, like it was something that actually happened."

Confused and somewhat irritated by what the woman had just spoken, Jacob stammered, "Uh . . . I don't know what you are talking about . . . and . . .I certainly don't know who you are."

The mysterious woman stood up from her chair. Her blond hair was long and flowing and the black jumpsuit she wore was very form-fitting, not leaving much to the imagination. Jacob was astounded by how statuesque and shapely she was.

Reaching out her hand as she sauntered toward Jacob in her stiletto heels. "Excuse my rudeness . . . my name is Lucinda. I am with Diablo Publishing. I must tell you, Doctor Prophitt, you are a hard man to get in contact with. I have called and emailed you on several occasions."

Jacob reluctantly shook her hand, "What are you referring to about my imagination?"

"The book you authored . . . you know . . . 'The Words of the Prophets' . . . I think it's hilarious!"

Expectantly a huge shock wave went down Jacob's spine and he immediately blurted out, "HILARIOUS! WHAT DO YOU MEAN BY HILARIOUS? That is a book referencing what I researched about the Prophets of Biblical times; it's not meant to be a comedy that was written to amuse the likes of you!"

Lucinda returned to her chair, sat down and slowly crossed her legs alluringly. "Oh, calm down Doctor Prophitt.

We are both exceedingly intelligent people here. You know as well as I do that it was highly unlikely that these so-called prophets really foretold anything. Those are all folklore that have been blown way out of proportion over the centuries. Even if those prophets ever existed, they were likely social misfits who were spurned by society. They were supposedly running around prophesying this and prophesying that, talking about an Almighty God that they conjured up in their own minds, who was going to do this and do that if the people didn't obey Him. I'm guessing that annoyed a lot of people." Lucinda chuckled at her own comment and continued, "We both know that the existence of a God in Heaven, the Creator of Heaven and Earth, is highly unlikely. I can reference a lengthy list of world-renowned scientists that have concluded that God doesn't exist. They have pretty much proven that all this universe, and even life itself, comes from a 'Big Bang'. I can also spot what's in your heart, Doctor Prophitt. Even you have doubts about what you have written."

Jacob, feeling a twinge of guilt, took a seat in another lawn chair that had been placed across the campfire from where she was sitting. "So, if you think I'm such a 'hack' as an author, why in the world would you risk life and limb up here in the woods at dusk to have a meeting with me?"

Lucinda reared back her head and gave out an evil laugh. "Trust me Doctor Prophitt . . . there isn't anything in these woods that I'm afraid of. As far as me thinking you're a 'hack' . . . quite the contrary . . . I think you're a genius. Anyone who can take legends and lore, claim considerable research on the subject, and then interpret the so-called prophesies and have a bunch of self-righteous, Bible-thumping scholastic types clamoring over your work, really impresses me. You know, my friend . . . with your talent and my influence, you could accomplish anything you want in this world."

THE WORDS OF A PROPHITT

Jacob, now fidgeting in his seat, was being both suspicious and interested at the same time in what Lucinda was saying. "But Miss . . . uh, I didn't get your last name."

"Just call me Lucinda."

"Uh, Lucinda . . . I haven't even given thought of another subject to write about. I'm not even sure I can come up with something that would interest anyone. 'The Words of the Prophets' was the result of a college thesis to get my PH.D. It just happened. I don't have any idea of where I would go from that."

Lucinda leaned forward in her seat, rested her elbows on her legs, clasped her hands over her knees and glared directly into Jacob's eyes. Jacob noticed that her blue eyes were now brighter . . . almost glowing . . . and her voice was sounding eviler . . . making him feel even more uncomfortable. "Doctor Prophitt, I'm not concerned about subject matter. I have tons of that available. What I want is your talent. If you were to put as much of an effort into writing more books as you did on the first one, you would become a huge celebrity in the theology world. You could write your own ticket. It could make you a very wealthy man."

Jacob arose from his chair and walked around behind it, facing her. "I think you misjudge me Lucinda. Being a wealthy person isn't a high priority in my life."

Lucinda got up from her chair and walked around the campfire to where Jacob was standing. When she reached him, she put her right hand on his shoulder, then walked around him with her hand trailing across his back, over his other shoulder to his chest, while the whole time looking him up and down. When she spoke again her voice returned to normal, "Mmm . . . you have potential. You're a tall drink of water Doctor Prophitt . . . and lean at that. If we shave off that horrid beard, get you a decent haircut, and get rid of that stupid ponytail I could turn you into an Adonis." She then leaned in toward his ear and whispered, "You're a man Doctor Prophitt . . . don't tell me you don't desire other women." Lucinda then stepped back and turned to face Jacob. "You could have beautiful women clambering after you . . . they'd be at your beck and call."

Jacob backed away from Lucinda to create more space between them. "I don't need other women . . . I'm in love with my wife."

Lucinda tilted her head back and let out another evil laugh, countering, "Honestly Doctor Prophitt? I personally feel that monogamy is highly overrated. You need to experience a little fun in your life. You can't tell me that on all those late nights working on your thesis that you weren't tempted to visit a forbidden website for a little eye candy . . . am I right?"

Jacob felt another twinge of guilt, and then anger. "I don't know what you are trying to pull here Lucinda! You're not gaining any ground with me talking like this!"

Lucinda walked over to the edge of the clearing overlooking Jacob's home, then turned to face Jacob again. "Alright . . . I guess I'm dealing with a boy scout. How about this; what about your broken little boy? You call him Zeke, don't you?"

Jacob, now highly agitated, retorted, "Yeah . . . what about Zeke? What in the hell do you know about my son?"

Lucinda sauntered back over to Jacob, placed her hand on his shoulder again, looked directly into his eyes with a concerned look. "Well, I know he has an incurable disease and is likely not long for this world. Just think, Doctor Prophitt . . . if you were very wealthy, you could take Zeke to the finest specialists in the world rather than dealing with these local, general practitioners who are only guessing at what they are doing. Highly trained specialists could likely prolong Zeke's life, even to the point of him carrying out what you put him on Earth to do."

"What do you mean by that statement?"

Lucinda ignored the question. "Doctor Prophitt . . . come here." She motioned to him as she walked back to the edge of the clearing. Jacob reluctantly followed her. Once he was standing by her, Lucinda directed him, "Look at this . . . it can all be yours." Suddenly . . . they were high above Earth! Jacob could even make out the curvature of the horizon. Beneath them he could see the lighting being emitted from all the major cities in North America. Suddenly, Jacob felt dizzy and was about to fall over the edge when Lucinda grabbed him and tucked her arm under his shoulder, pulling him close to her to steady him. "Doctor Prophitt, with my assistance you can become a huge star in the theology world. Because of your book you have credibility, and those who believe in the word of the fictional 'Almighty God' will listen to you. People will be waiting in anticipation of everything you say and do. With my inspiration and your talent, we together can literally change the course of history. Trust me Doctor Prophitt, I will take very good care of you."

Suddenly . . . out of nowhere Jacob heard another voice replying, "Said the snake . . . before filling you with venom!"

Jacob spun around to see a familiar face standing next to the campfire. "Mister D'Angelo . . . uh, Michael! Where did you come from? What are you doing here?"

"Oh, I was just in the neighborhood and detected a disturbance and a horrible stench in the atmosphere. So, I thought I would stop by and make sure you didn't make a huge mistake."

Lucinda released her hold on Jacob, strode across the clearing returning to her lawn chair. With a sneer on her face, she responded with a terse comment, "Ah, Michael . . . you're a poor excuse for a 'being'. It's been a long time. So, how's Yahweh's favorite go-fer?"

Jacob, now standing alone at the edge of the clearing, turned back expecting to look out over the world again, only to see the rooftops and streetlights of his neighborhood below him. Slowly and cautiously he backed away from the edge of the clearing. Michael, taking a seat in the lawn chair where Jacob had sat before replied, "It has been a long time . . . but not long enough. I was doing fine until running into you. Why don't you go back to the sewer you crawled out of and leave Doc alone? He's doing alright without the likes of you coming around and meddling in his life."

Jacob noticed that Michael and Lucinda's eyes were beginning to glow brighter as they were staring at each other. Being both scared and confused, Jacob blurted out, "What in the hell is going on here?"

Michael, speaking without breaking his glare at Lucinda, answered, "Doc, she . . . or rather 'that' is not what she appears to be. You, my friend, have come face to face with the 'Prince of Darkness'. Her name is not Lucinda. It's 'Lucifer', or 'Beelzebub', or 'The Devil'. Whatever you choose, it's all the same. She, or rather 'It', is attempting to get you to sell your soul for wealth, notoriety, and hard telling what else. But I can promise you this . . . whatever is being offered will result in your soul living in eternal damnation."

Lucinda was visibly becoming more irritated with what Michael was saying. When she spoke, her voice was sounding even more evil. "Ah Michael . . . you do have a way with women, don't you? At least I look better than you. I can't believe you are parading around as an over-the-hill, has-been, with a pot-belly. So, tell all of us here, what do you have to offer that is going to make Doctor Prophitt's life better? Is it him knowing that the 'Almighty God' exists, even though that God is not willing to do anything for what's-his-name?"

Michael bellowed an answer that rang out through the woods. "It's Ezekiel, you idiot! You don't even know the kid's name!"

"Yeah, I know his name! Answer my question! What can you provide that's better than what I am offering? At least with my way he can enjoy the fruits of life, rather than living a paltry existence and sitting by watching his son die a slow death to an early grave."

Michael's eyes began glowing even brighter. "What I can offer Jacob is having a pleasurable life here on Earth, as well as knowing that once he moves on to the hereafter, he will be with the ones he loves including, finally being with his mother, in paradise. A real plus is that he won't have to go through eternity with the smell of burning Sulphur in his nose and with you mocking him every day for following 'you' into Hell!"

With the glow in their eyes becoming increasingly intense, both Michael and Lucinda stood up, glaring at each other across the campfire. Terrified with disbelief, Jacob started moving backwards toward his bicycle, planning an escape, stammering, "Uh . . . guys . . . I am going to go now . . . I'll leave so you two can continue this discussion without me."

Michael and Lucinda, with their eyes now flaming, glared at Jacob and yelled out in unison, "DON'T MOVE . . . I'LL BE RIGHT BACK WITH YOU!" Jacob froze, afraid to move a muscle, but did reach behind him to feel how close his bicycle was in case he needed to make a run for it.

Michael turned back to face Lucinda, "It's time for you to leave Lucifer. There's nothing here for you."

Lucinda, now speaking with the evil voice of a man, responded, "You moron, I'm not going anywhere until I have this guy's soul. Why don't you take your sorry-self off this mountain and let me finish what I came here for?"

Michael, now speaking in a totally different voice, countered, "There is no way in Heaven's name that you are taking Doc's soul. I have orders from a much higher power than you to protect him at all costs."

Lucinda was quiet for a moment, staring intently at Michael. Then she inquired, "So, does 'at all costs' mean even the end of your existence?"

"If necessary."

"Fine! Let's end this, here and now!"

"Fine! I'm ready!

The intense glow from both of their eyes was now lighting the evening sky, making it look like it was daytime. Simultaneously Jacob heard thunder roll through the Smoky Mountains and he watched in horror as Michael and Lucinda suddenly transformed into enormous warriors facing each other, wielding huge swords and shields ready for battle, yelling at each other in a language that Jacob did not recognize. Suddenly the campfire between the titans exploded into the sky, towering over the clearing. The concussion from the explosion knocked Jacob back, causing him to fall over his bicycle and hit the ground hard beside it. The fall caused a sharp pain in his left hip that took his breath away. While lying on the ground attempting to regain his sense of equilibrium, unable to get back on his feet, Jacob looked over to see what was happening at the campfire when a booming voice came out of the heavens, shaking the earth under him, "MICHAEL! IT IS NOT TIME!"

The combatants stopped. Michael reverently obeyed. "As you say." He then knelt on one knee, laid his sword and shield on the ground and bowed down before Lucinda. Once Michael had done that, he began to shrink back to his original size, with Lucinda towering over him, ready to strike with her sword.

After a tense pause, Lucinda yelled out, "DAMMIT! I DON'T WANT IT TO HAPPEN THIS WAY!" Then she also began shrinking, returning to her original form. "When I finish you off, I want it to be a battle, not a slaughter."

Then the booming voice echoed from the heavens again, "BE GONE, LUCIFER!"

Lucinda immediately began scurrying around, picking up her lawn chair and the book she was reading and then headed for the woods. She stopped and turned toward Michael, "This isn't over Michael! We *will* meet again!"

Michael stood up facing her, "True, this isn't over. I look forward to the outcome . . . you know what is written."

Lucinda exclaimed with another evil laugh. "Michael, blow it out your . . ." Her final words were drowned out by another clap of thunder and then she was gone.

The campfire had now diminished and Michael was standing next to it, deep in thought, when he heard a loud moan from the edge of the clearing. Turning around toward Jacob, he blurted out, "Oh . . . hey, Doc. I'm sorry, I forgot all about you." Picking up the lawn chair he was standing next to, Michael carried it over and set it down close to where Jacob was lying on the ground next to his bicycle. Michael sat down and inquired, "Are you alright?"

"NO! I'm not alright! I think I've broken my hip! I can't get up! It hurts really bad."

"Gee, Doc . . . that's tough. Man, you Jacob guys have a thing about injuring your hips. I remember a few centuries ago when the Boss wrestled with . . ."

"Yeah . . . I know the story. Do something to help me here. I've got to get up and get home. It's dark now."

"Oh, Doc . . . I don't think you're going to be riding home anytime soon. You need to lie there and take it easy. I'm sure somebody will be looking for you in a little while."

Jacob lay his head back on the ground in frustration with Michael. "You're an angel, aren't you?"

Michael started laughing, "What makes you think I'm an angel Doc?"

Raising back up on an elbow, looking at Michael, Jacob answered, "I saw how you transformed into a giant a little while ago. How do you explain that?"

"Oh . . . you saw that? I guess you were here, weren't you?"

Jacob lay back down looking up at the sky. Moaning loudly from the pain, he responded, "Yeah, I saw that. So, now that I know you're an angel, fix my hip so I can go home to my family."

"No can do, Doc. That stuff is way above my pay grade. You're gonna have to be patient."

Jacob, with the pain in his hip increasing and realizing that he was getting nowhere with Michael, decided to change the subject. "So, tell me Michael, was that who I think it was in the flame?"

Michael shifted in his chair getting more comfortable before responding. "So . . . Doc, who do you think it was?"

"Don't toy with me Michael. I'm in a lot of pain here. Okay, I'll just say it . . . God Almighty, Yahweh, The Man upstairs . . . is He real?"

Michael got up from his chair and began doing stretching exercises, as if he was preparing to play golf, which was annoying Jacob. "Well, unless you are deaf, I am pretty sure you heard His voice in the fire. I would say He's certainly real. The Boss will make an occasional personal appearance down here, and when He does, He likes to make a huge production of it. That fire thing was pretty cool, wasn't it?"

Jacob, now getting more incensed by the second, struggled to get back up on an elbow so he could look at Michael while speaking. "Okay, so God exists. Why does He hate me?"

Michael stopped stretching and stood motionless for a moment looking as if he was deep in thought. "Doc, the Boss doesn't hate you . . . in fact he has taken a special interest in you."

"If He has taken this so-called special interest in me, why hasn't He answered my prayers?"

Michael returned to the lawn chair and sat down, leaning over to be close to Jacob. "Doc, He did answer your prayers . . . He gave you a son."

"My son has a horrible disease and he is getting worse every day. I've prayed to your 'Boss' for healing and He has ignored my prayers." Jacob now saw an expression on Michael's face that he hadn't seen since he talked about the thirteenth hole at Augusta National while in front of the diner . . . an expression of sincerity.

Michael leaned back in his chair, looking directly into Jacob's eyes, "See . . . there is the problem. You must understand that the Boss knows everything that is in your heart. You can't hide anything from Him. Jacob, you should be totally honest with yourself when praying to God. In your mind, you were praying for Ezekiel's life . . . but down in the deepest, darkest recesses of your heart, you were praying for the continuation of your family's legacy."

Jacob lay back down, looking up at the stars in the sky. The pain in his hip was now overtaken by the pain he felt in his heart. Tears started rolling out of his eyes and he put his hands up to his face, sobbing loudly into the night. After a brief time, Jacob put down his hands and looked up at Michael. "Oh God . . . Michael, I've really screwed things up. What can I do?"

Michael got up from his chair and returned to doing his stretching exercises. "I wouldn't worry too much about it Doc. The Boss is pretty good at giving out second chances. You'll figure out something, I'm sure. Anyway, I've got to hit the road. I have an early tee-time at Augusta National in the morning."

The pain in Jacob's hip suddenly increased and he let out a prolonged moan, and begged, "Michael! Don't leave me here alone. I'm in excruciating pain and I can't help myself. Do something!"

Michael returned to his chair to be close to Jacob. "Don't worry Doc, someone will be here shortly. Here, let's try this until they do. I want you to relax . . . concentrate on your breathing. Now I want you to envision in your mind someplace that you would like to be right now . . . a happy place. Is it helping?"

"Yeah . . . a little."

"Okay then . . . now I want you to start counting backward from ten. Let's start. Ten . . . nine . . . you are getting more relaxed . . . eight . . . seven . . . six . . . take another deep breath . . . five . . . four . . .

CHAPTER TWELVE

JACOB WAS AWAKENED IN NEARLY total darkness by the hum of engines and several voices calling out his name. "MISTER PROPHITT! JACOB PROPHITT! CAN YOU HEAR US MISTER PROPHITT? JACOB, WHERE ARE YOU?"

He recognized the last voice as that of Rebecca. Looking around from where he was lying, he saw that his biking helmet was within reach, so he grabbed it, turned on the flashlight and began shining it in the air. "I'M OVER . . . OWWWW!" Jacob was immediately reminded of the pain in his hip when he tried to yell out. Speaking out much less intensely, "I'm over here. Can you hear me?" He then lay still, listening for a response.

In the distance he heard, "I SAW A LIGHT UP IN THE CLEARING!" Shortly, a large group of people carrying flashlights and lanterns came riding up on all-terrain vehicles to where he was lying. Surrounding him, they began asking all sorts of questions at the same time. "Doctor Prophitt, are you alright? Are you able to get up on your feet? Are you in pain?" And then Rebecca, moving people out of her way, knelt next to him, "Jacob, what in the world are you doing up here this time of night?"

Then a voice, which Jacob did not recognize, rang out above the commotion. "OKAY EVERYONE! LET'S ALL BACK AWAY AND LET ME ASSESS THE SITUATION HERE! Rebecca moved away, and another person with a lantern moved in close to Jacob. Jacob immediately noticed he was wearing a police uniform. "Okay Mister Prophitt, I'm Sheriff Finch with the police department. May I call you Jacob?"

Jacob, now finding it painful to even talk, just nodded in the affirmative in response to Sheriff Finch's question.

"Fine. Now Jacob, are you injured?"

Jacob again nodded yes.

"Can you tell me where you hurt?"

Speaking softly, Jacob answered, "It's my left hip. I think it might be broken."

"Alright, that answers that question." Sheriff Finch turned looking back at someone else behind him, "Andy, get on the radio and get the EMT's up here. Tell them to bring a four-wheeler and a backboard so we can transport Mister Prophitt off this hill. Also, tell them they will probably need a strong pain killer so he can stand the trip down. Have them check with the ER and see what they can do. One of you other guys take Misses Prophitt back down the hill to her house, so she can get to the hospital to meet us there."

Rebecca again knelt close to Jacob and touched him on the cheek, "Now Jacob do what these gentlemen tell you to do. I've worked with them on several occasions at the hospital and they know what they are doing. Okay?" Jacob didn't reply, he merely nodded in agreement. Rebecca, with a concerned look, patted him on the chest, stood up and left with one of the other officers.

Sheriff Finch returned, shining his lantern in Jacob's eyes. "So, Jacob, what were you doing up here this time of night? It's not too smart to be riding in these woods after dark."

Jacob brought his hand up to shade the light from his eyes. "I got up here much earlier. It wasn't this dark when I rode into the clearing. I thought I saw a campfire burning and came up here to check it out. I thought it might be some students up here partying."

"So, was anybody up here?"

"Yeah, there was some woman I didn't know. Apparently, she had been trying to get in touch with me and I guess she decided the best way to do that was to entice me up here so she could talk with me."

"And was there a campfire?"

"Yeah, there was a campfire and a couple of lawn chairs. No, wait a minute, I think she took her chair with her when she left."

Sheriff Finch stood up and instructed, "Stay put. I'm gonna look around."

Jacob snorted, "I'm not going anywhere right now."

Finch let out a little laugh, "Yeah, I guess you aren't. Boys, let's fan out and look around this clearing. Jacob here says there was a campfire burning when he got here." Then Finch walked out of Jacob's sight. It was quiet for a few minutes and then Jacob noticed that all the officers had formed in a huddle near him and were talking in muffled voices. Finally, Sheriff Finch returned and knelt next to Jacob. "So, Jacob, tell me, did you partake in any alcoholic beverages before you took off on this little adventure of yours?"

Jacob retorted, "NO! Absolutely not!"

"Well then, let me ask you this . . . have you recently taken any prescription drugs, or maybe non-prescription drugs . . . if you get my drift . . . that might have made you hallucinate?"

Jacob was now getting exceedingly irritated. "Absolutely not! I don't use any sort of drugs other than an occasional over-the-counter cold medicine. What are you getting at anyway?"

"Well, Jacob . . . we don't see anything that would indicate that anyone else was ever up here. There's no evidence of a campfire and not even a blade of grass that has been disturbed"

Jacob laid his head back on the ground and moaned. "Oh no . . . not again!"

"So, Jacob . . . what did you mean by that?"

"Sheriff, it's a long story and you wouldn't understand."

"Give me a chance Jacob. I might surprise you."

"No, Sheriff Finch, it's too far-fetched. I think I'm better off not giving you an explanation right now."

"Well, Jacob, just to be sure, I'll have someone come back up in the daylight and scour the area, but I don't think we'll find anything. You were either dreaming, or hallucinating on something. I'm gonna order a blood test on you to make sure. I don't appreciate being sent out on wild goose chases by guys like you putting my people at risk."

Jacob was ready to argue his case, but then thought better of it and decided to lay still and close his eyes to try to lessen his discomfort. Just then he heard another vehicle making its way up the trail. When it entered the clearing, Officer Finch instructed, "Okay guys, let's back away from Jacob, but keep the lights pointed on him so the medics can see what they are doing."

As soon as Sheriff Finch moved away, a somewhat familiar face came into Jacob's sight. The person placed a medical bag next to him and spoke in a cheerful voice, "Hi Doctor Prophitt. How are you doing? I'm Mitch with the fire department. I'm here to get you off this hill."

Jacob squinted, attempting to focus on the fireman's face. "Mitch, don't I know you?"

"Yes sir! I'm in your class at the University."

Jacob laid his head back on the ground and replied, "Ah . . . I thought I knew you. I didn't know you were on the fire department."

Mitch chuckled. "Hey, I've got to pay my tuition somehow. Okay, this is what we are going to do. The ER doc has prescribed a pain medicine to numb you up so we can get off this hill. I'm going to give you an IV; it should deaden the pain very fast. You might start feeling a little loopy when the medicine enters your system, but you should stay coherent. Once the pain eases, these fine gentlemen are going to move you onto a backboard and strap you down real secure. Then we're going to load you onto a four-wheel-drive vehicle that we call a 'mule'. It has a bed on the back like a truck. We will make sure you are secure in the bed and then we work our way down the hill to the ambulance. I'm going to be with you until we get to the hospital, so you need to let me know if you start feeling any discomfort while we make our way down. Any questions?"

Jacob moved his head back and forth indicating that he didn't. "Okay, Doctor Prophitt, let's get this ball rolling." Mitch opened his medical bag and pulled out a needle, a bottle of alcohol, and cotton swabs. He then searched for a vein to put the IV in. After swabbing the area Mitch hesitated. "Okay, Doctor Prophitt, this might sting a little. Are you ready?"

Jacob nodded his understanding and immediately felt a prick in his arm. Mitch attached the IV to the needle in Jacob's arm and within a few seconds Jacob noticed a burning sensation and tingling all over his body. A few moments later, the pain subsided and he felt like he was having some kind of out-of-body experience. Mitch, still sitting next to Jacob inquired, "How are you feeling Doctor Prophitt? Do you have any pain?"

Jacob, now starting to feel giddy, giggled, "I'm feeling much better now!" He continued giggling like a little child.

Mitch took that as the answer he needed. "Okay guys, we're ready. I'm going to strap Doctor Prophitt's legs together to attempt to immobilize his left hip. Then we are going to gently roll him over on his right side and slide the backboard under him and then roll him over on the board and strap him down, so we can put him on the back of the 'mule'. Jacob could hear all the discussions and see the people working around him. He then felt himself being rolled on his side and then rolled back over on the board. It all seemed well orchestrated with Mitch directing every move. After a few more moments, he felt himself being lifted on the board and loaded onto the four-wheeler. Mitch returned within Jacob's view again. "Doctor Prophitt, we are ready to head down the trail. I can't ride with you, but I will be right alongside you on foot. If you feel any discomfort let me know."

Again, Jacob giggled. "Sure Mitch!"

Mitch laughed out loud announcing, "Okay guys, I don't think he's feeling any pain. Let's move it!"

Jacob felt the 'mule' moving as they began descending the hill on the trail. They were moving at a snail's pace to keep the ride as smooth as possible and Jacob was thinking it was going to take all night to reach the bottom. Jacob was coherent enough to understand what Mitch was saying. When Mitch would ask how he was doing, Jacob was able to respond. At the same time, Jacob was going back over the events of the evening in his mind, questioning himself about whether this was real, or was he hallucinating like Officer Finch suggested? Was Lucinda truly Satan? Did he really hear the voice of God in the campfire? Then he decided that maybe he needed to visit a psychiatrist and sort these things out because no one else would believe what had been going on in his life. A shrink might even consider having him committed if he shared the events in the past weeks while on the couch.

Before he could move on to his next thought, Mitch touched his arm, "We're here Doctor Prophitt. Are you feeling any pain yet?" Jacob gestured no with his head rather than speaking. "Okay then. We're going to move you onto a gurney and then put you in the ambulance, so we can get you to the hospital." While everyone was preparing to move him, Jacob was looking around and could see faint images of curious bystanders through the flashing red and blue lights of the ambulance and police cars. They were watching the action from the edge of the road. Feeling somewhat embarrassed, he stared up at the sky to avoid making eye contact with anyone. Jacob felt himself being lifted out of the 'mule' and onto the gurney, then quickly wheeled over to the ambulance. Next, he felt the lunge as the gurney legs collapsed under it as it was pushed into the back of the ambulance. Mitch immediately jumped in and sat down next to Jacob. As the doors slammed shut, Mitch pounded on the back of the cab yelling at the driver, "Okay . . . hit the road! We're ready back here!" Jacob felt the ambulance pull onto the street and could hear the sirens blasting through the night as they headed toward the hospital. Jacob felt Mitch's hand touch his shoulder. "You still alright Doctor Prophitt?" Jacob gave him a nod indicating he was. "Okay, hang in there, we'll be at the hospital very shortly."

Jacob had dozed off during the ride but was awakened when the ambulance doors were flung open and there was suddenly a flurry of activity all around him. As he was rolled into the emergency room, people came from all directions. He could tell he was being pushed down a corridor and then wheeled into a cubicle where a group of orderlies and nurses began attending to him. He was unstrapped from the backboard and lifted onto the hospital bed in the room. Mitch came to his side, "Okay Doctor Prophitt, this is the end of the road for me. I'll check on you later to see how you are doing."

Then he was gone, and two nurses began taking Jacob's vitals. Jacob was somewhat familiar with both of them since they worked with Rebecca. One of them spoke up, "Are you in any discomfort Doctor Prophitt?"

"Uh . . . the drugs are beginning to wear off. I'm beginning to feel some pain in my hip."

"Alright, I will notify Doctor Griffin. He will be with you as soon as he is finished looking at another patient."

The two nurses left the cubicle and Rebecca appeared at his side and immediately questioned him, "Jacob Prophitt! What in the hell were you doing riding in the woods in the dark of night? You could have been killed!"

Jacob reached for her hand and then looked around the room to see if anyone else was there. "Rebecca, I was in the presence of God tonight."

"Jacob! What are you talking about? Why were you up on that hill?"

"I'm trying to tell you Rebecca . . . I saw a campfire burning and I went up to check it out. That Lucinda lady who has been leaving all the voicemails on our phone was there. She lured me up there to talk to me. It turns out that she is the Devil, Lucifer. I was face-to-face with Satan himself, or herself, whatever. But remember that D'Angelo guy I told you about? He showed up also. It turns out he's an angel. The two of them were prepared to battle for my soul when

God appeared in the fire and stopped them. I heard the voice of God Rebecca! I really did!"

Rebecca, with a serious and concerned look, patted Jacob on the chest. "Jacob, you've had a rough night. Lie back and rest and Doctor Griffin will be in to look at you. I will be right here."

"You don't believe a word I said, do you?"

"Jacob, just rest. We can talk more about it tomorrow. Okay?"

Jacob decided it was useless to continue so he closed his eyes, still rehashing the last few hours. Then another thought came to mind. "Rebecca, where are the kids?"

Rebecca moved away from the bed and sat in a chair in the cubicle. "Aaron and Mindy Weiss are watching them. They are helping with their homework and making sure they go to bed. They are staying at our house until I get home."

"Oh, that's very nice of them."

Rebecca sighed, "Yes, it is. It's nice to have neighbors we can trust at times like this."

Soon Jacob heard another voice enter the room and recognized it as Doctor Griffin, their family doctor. "So, Jacob Prophitt . . . I understand that you have been riding your little bicycle through the woods again. I would have thought you would have gotten over that, now that you're a big-time college professor!" The doctor grabbed the chart off the end of the bed and began reviewing it, speaking to Jacob without looking up, "So you're having a hip issue. Tell me what happened."

"I fell backward over my bike and landed on my left hip. It feels like it's broken."

Doctor Griffin continued to look down at the chart. "Well Jacob, you're pretty fit. I doubt that a fall on the ground would be enough to break your hip. You haven't reached that age yet. We'll take some pictures up in 'x-ray' and see what's going on." Then Doctor Griffin hung the chart back on the end of the bed and moved to Jacob's bedside looking sternly at him. "I have an order from the Sherriff's Department for a toxicology blood test. I need to inform you of your rights. You can refuse to let me do this, but it can result in the automatic suspension of your driver's license if you do so. So, what do you want to do?"

"Go ahead Doc. There isn't anything they are going to find anyway, except maybe alfalfa sprouts."

"Good! Nurse draw some blood and I'll notify 'x-ray' that he will be on his way up." Then he turned his attention to Rebecca. "I want you to go home and rest. I will let you know what we find out. I'll give you a call shortly, before it gets too late. You know we'll take good care of your husband."

Rebecca got up and walked over to Jacob. She gave him a kiss on the forehead and then with a tired smile told him, "I will see you later honey. You're in good hands. Good night." She turned to leave and then stopped in the hallway. "Doctor Griffin. Can I have a word with you out here?" Doctor Griffin followed her down the hall and she stopped when she was far enough away, so Jacob couldn't hear the conversation.

Doctor Griffin questioned, "What is it Rebecca?"

"Doctor, Jacob was talking crazy to me a few minutes ago . . . talking about hearing the voice of God and being face-to-face with Satan. I'm afraid he might have experienced some head trauma. Please check him over."

Doctor Griffin put his hand on Rebecca's shoulder, to reassure her. "Being a nurse, you know that people react differently to medications. Jacob might be one of those that isn't able to handle the pain medicine we gave him very well. That might be the reason he's talking that way. But we will check him out to make sure. Now go home and get some rest."

Rebecca replied with an exhausted smile, "Thank you Doctor Griffin." She then turned and continued down the hall to the exit and left the building.

Doctor Griffin returned to Jacob. "Okay Jacob, we are going up to 'x-ray'. I will meet you there."

Two orderlies came in and rolled Jacob out of the cubicle and down the hall to the elevators. From that moment on, it seemed to Jacob like an eternity. It was "hurry up and wait" for everything. Once the x-rays were done, he was moved back to the cubicle in the emergency room where he was left alone for what seemed like hours, looking at, but not really watching, what was on the television on the wall. He could not help but hear the ambulance sirens as they pulled into the hospital, hear the moans of sick and injured people coming and going, and noticing the muffled conversations out in the hallway, apparently between doctors and family members of the patients. He thought back on the events of the evening, beginning to doubt if they really had happened. Between the pain medication and tiredness along with total boredom, Jacob finally went to sleep.

"Jacob! Jacob!" Jacob was awakened by someone shaking his shoulder. He looked up and saw it was Doctor Griffin. "Jacob, this is Doctor Breeden. He is our orthopedic surgeon here at the hospital. He is going to explain to you what we found and what we are going to do."

Jacob, still in a little fog, looked over at a gentleman who appeared to be in his sixties, short in stature, with gray hair. The doctor held out his hand to shake Jacob's. "Hi Jacob. I am Doctor Breeden. I consulted with Doctor Griffin regarding your condition. After reviewing the x-rays, we have determined that you have a dislocated hip. What we are going to do now is move you into the OR where we have a solid surface to work on and put your hip back in place. We are going to put you under anesthesia, so we can manipulate your hip without any pain to you. It won't take long, but you will be out for a while, so you will be spending the night here at the hospital. Any questions?"

Jacob looked at Doctor Griffin. "Is Rebecca aware of all this?"

"Yes, she is. I just got off the phone with her. She has been consulted and approves."

"Alright, let's do it and get it over with."

"Okay Jacob, I will send the nurse in with the consent forms for you to sign and Doctor Breeden and I will see you inthe OR." Both doctors left the cubicle and the nurse walked in with the forms. Once that was done, the orderlies returned for Jacob to take him for another trip to the elevators. After the short trip to another floor of the hospital, Jacob was wheeled into a sterile looking room with a lot of bright lights. The orderlies and nurses lifted him off the gurney onto a hard metal table. Once he was there, several people began hooking him up to different machines, making sure they were working properly. Shortly, the two doctors and assisting nurses arrived and stood around the table. Doctor Griffin spoke, "Jacob the anesthesiologist is ready. Do you have any questions? Jacob answered no by shaking his head. "Alright, let's get started. Good night Jacob."

CHAPTER THIRTEEN

JACOB OPENED HIS EYES AND found himself in an unfamiliar room with the sun shining brightly through the windows. He was still groggy from the anesthesia but was slowly gaining his coherency. Suddenly, from the side of his bed he heard, "Good mornin' sunshine. How ya'll doin'? Jacob immediately recognized the voice and turned his head to see Rabbi Weiss sitting in a chair, leafing through a magazine. Aaron, without looking up, continued, "It's a beautiful mornin' out there. Too bad yer missin' it."

Jacob turned his head back, looking toward the ceiling. "How long have you been here?"

"Not long. Maybe an hour or so. I wanted to be here when you woke up."

"Why is that?"

"Well . . . I was hopin' that we could talk. Rebecca was all stressed out when she got home last night about some crazy talk you were doin'. So, I thought I would stop in and see what's goin' on."

Jacob continued lying flat on his back, looking up at the ceiling, refusing to look at his visitor. "Aaron, there is no sense in sharing this with you. The Sherriff thinks I was hallucinating and even my own wife thinks I've gone crazy. This whole thing is so farfetched; I'm afraid I will get the same response from you. What's the use in discussing this?"

Aaron arose from his chair and pulled it over, closer to the hospital bed. "Try me."

Jacob hesitated, and then asked, "How do I know you won't share what I tell you with someone else?"

"Jacob, I'm a Rabbi and a licensed counselor. I have to uphold client/counselor privilege. I wouldn't be able to divulge our conversation with Mindy, even if she were to put me in a headlock. Maybe I can help ya'll shed some light on what happened."

Jacob laid motionless for a few more moments. He then reached for the control to the hospital bed, raising his head up to get a better view of Aaron. "I'm still not sure about this Aaron."

"Go ahead Jacob! What ya got to lose? Ya might even gain some sanity." Then Aaron laughed softly.

Jacob, not thinking that last statement was very funny, released a huge sigh. "I wouldn't even know where to begin."

Aaron leaned back in his chair appearing to be preparing for a long discussion. "I suggest ya start at the beginnin'. We both have all day with nothin' else goin' on."

Jacob continued to stare at the ceiling, remaining quiet. After a few moments, he began, "This whole thing started on the day you and I met. After we had coffee, I went to the classroom to prepare for class. I walked into the classroom and found a guy up on the top tier, slumped in his chair napping. I said something about him being very early, and he just waved me off. During the class, he was being disruptive. He kept snoring very loud, and all the students kept laughing. After the class, I admonished him, but he explained that he wasn't a student. He said he was there to observe me."

Aaron leaned forward in his chair. "Observe ya doin' what?"

"I don't know. He just said that his boss sent him to observe me."

Aaron, now more intent, asked, "What was his name?"

"It was Michael."

"Michael what?"

"Michael D'Angelo."

Aaron sat back in his chair tapping his chin with his finger. "Hmmmm . . . interesting."

Jacob, peering over at Aaron with a curious look responded, "Hmmm what? Do you know this guy?"

"Heard of him . . . can't say I've had the pleasure.

Jacob scoffed at Aaron's comment. "Hah! Believe me, he's not a pleasure. I made the mistake of going to lunch with D'Angelo and he embarrassed me in front of the whole diner. And what's worse, Dean Howard was there, and D'Angelo made fun of his choice of attire, commenting that he wanted to meet Howard's tailor." Then Jacob chuckled to himself. "In retrospect, that was kind of funny. Anyway, then he proceeded to give the waitress an incredibly crazy amount of money for a tip and shrugged it off like it was nothing. Then he goes out to get in his car, after telling me his boss was big into saving the environment, and he's driving a big black gashog and claims it runs on water right out of a garden hose. It was all so surreal." Jacob then became silent and returned to staring at the ceiling.

Aaron waited for a few moments before prodding Jacob for more information. "Did ya see this Michael guy again?"

Jacob came out of his trance and looked over at Aaron. "Uh . . . no . . . I didn't see him anymore . . . at least I think not until last night." Then Jacob went silent again. Aaron got up from his chair and walked over to the window, looking out over the landscape, waiting for Jacob to continue. Then, after what seemed to Aaron to be an eternity, Jacob spoke up, "So after the diner, I went to Dean Howard's for the 'meet-and-greet' where, as you know, I encountered President Upton, who was intent on having 'the talk' with me." Jacob then returned his gaze to Aaron. "That conversation had to be one of the most unusual things I have sat through in my life. Aaron, he was all over the place on every subject that he discussed. It was unbelievable!"

Aaron laughed, then returned to his chair next to Jacob's bed. "Trust me Jacob, almost all the current faculty here at the University has had to endure what I'm sure was a similar conversation with President Upton. I certainly wouldn't put too much thought into that."

Before Aaron could say another word, there was a knock on the door and then it swung open. A nurse dressed in bright pink scrubs, her face beaming with a huge smile, burst into the room. "Good morning Doctor Prophitt! I'm Sandy, I'll be your attending nurse today. I'm so glad to see that you're awake. Open your mouth and place this under your tongue." The nurse immediately shoved a thermometer into Jacob's mouth, then asked, "How are you feeling?" Jacob could only nod and mumble his answer. She then grabbed his arm and began checking his pulse. "Doctor Griffin said he will be in to check on you early this afternoon to see how you are doing." Nurse Sandy continued with her examination by placing a blood pressure cuff on Jacob's arm while she was still talking at warp speed. "I saw your wife as I was coming in this morning. She's on another floor today, but she said she would stop by to check on you when she's finished with her morning rounds. Are you feeling any pain or discomfort?" Again, Jacob could only answer by shaking his head and mumbling his answer because of the thermometer still stuck in his mouth. She began pumping the blood pressure cuff on his arm and continued, "It's going to be another beautiful day here in the Smoky Mountains. It's a shame you must be inside all day. I love this time of year . . . don't you?" All Jacob could do was nod. "I'm not looking forward to winter coming. I hate winter . . . don't you?" Jacob again shook his head in response. Then Nurse Sandy became quiet as she checked his blood pressure; next she removed the thermometer from Jacob's mouth and read the results. Once she was finished, she went to the end of the hospital bed and pulled a chart out of its holder and began writing. She continued to be quiet while she was reviewing the information on the chart. Then the beaming smile returned. "Everything looks great in here. I hope you have a wonderful day! Just press the button on your remote if you need anything. We'll come running if you do. Goodbye Doctor Prophitt!" Then Nurse Sandy exited the room just a quickly as she entered.

Jacob and Aaron simultaneously looked at each other and suddenly broke out laughing. "Gee Jacob . . . I think ya'll just witnessed a pink tornado!" Both continued to chuckle for a moment, then Aaron returned to the conversation. "So . . . after your conversation with Upton what happened?"

Jacob rubbed his forehead, as if he was trying to remember, "Well, I went home and that was when I met your wife, Mindy. After Mindy left, Rebecca told me there was a voicemail message from a Lucinda with some publishing company. This Lucinda said she wanted to speak to me about my next project. I haven't even begun to have another project to work on, so I blew it off and didn't call her back. Later that evening I was sitting on the back porch and noticed for the first time at dusk what appeared to be a campfire up on the hill behind the house. I just figured it was students partying and dismissed it. From then on, I continued to get phone messages from this Lucinda, which I never returned, and I kept seeing what looked like a campfire up on the clearing."

Aaron shifted in his chair, getting more comfortable. "So, is that what led up to last night?"

Jacob paused before answering. "Oh, no! It gets a lot weirder from that point. I had this feeling deep down that there were a lot of things I didn't know about my family . . . more specifically about my mother. It just seemed like my father and grandfather were always hiding something from me, so I decided to take a road trip to Kentucky to see Grandpa Eli to get some answers."

Aaron leaned forward in his chair, now more intent on listening. "So, did ya learn anything?"

"Oh, yeah! I learned plenty!" Then Jacob gave out a little snicker, "The funniest part of the trip is I ran into President Upton's granddaughter working at a roadside stand in a small town on my way to Somerset."

Aaron sat back in his seat amazed. "No way! That's unreal! Was she anything like her grandfather?"

Jacob laughed, "No, she was able to stay on a subject!"

Aaron, still laughing at Jacob's comment, got up from his chair and returned to the window. While looking out the window, with his back to Jacob, he continued with his questioning. "So, tell me about weirder."

Jacob reached for the control to his bed and started adjusting it so his head would raise higher to get a better view of Aaron. As the bed was moving, he started feeling a twinge in his hip and decided not to sit up any further. After getting comfortable and gathering his thoughts, he continued, "Well, when I got to Grandpa Eli's, he immediately took me up to 'the point', a clearing on a ridge that lies above an artery of Cumberland Lake. While we were talking, I sort of had a meltdown. I started screaming out to high heaven.

THE WORDS OF A PROPHITT

For some reason my frustrations got the best of me and I let go in front of him. I was so embarrassed. I would never in my life thought of doing anything like that in front of my grandfather."

Aaron continued to stand at the window with his back to Jacob, seemingly disinterested in the conversation. Then he asked, "So, how did your grandfather react?"

"Well, unexpectantly, he calmly had me sit next to him on the bench and began to tell me about this affliction we Prophitt men have."

Aaron, still with his back to Jacob, prodded further, "So, what is this so-called affliction he was telling you about?"

Jacob took in a deep breath and began, "For generations, the Prophitt men have had this obsession with continuing our family legacy . . . the Prophitt name. So, as a result, we have all had five daughters in our attempt to have a son. Fortunately, we have all been successful at eventually having a son. The unfortunate part is that once the son was born, all the daughters had been ignored by the father in one way or another, causing animosity in the family between everyone. The daughters end up hating the son and the father because of the father's doting over his 'pride-and-joy'. So, we are all members of dysfunctional families. It's like there's a curse on the Prophitt men."

"So, tell me Jacob . . . is this so-called curse something you have experienced in your lifetime?"

Jacob lay quiet for a moment debating how to answer. "Well, Grandpa Eli told me he barely had any relationships with his sisters because of what his daddy did, and I know my aunts have almost nothing to do with Daddy. Grandpa Eli admitted to me that it was his fault. As far as my immediate family, things are different because I make every effort to treat the girls equally to my son. But there are some extenuating circumstances."

"And those extenuating circumstances are . . .?"

Jacob released an audible sigh, and speaking in frustration answered, "Aaron! I'm talking about Ezekiel! He probably won't live past his teens!"

"And that's why you're mad at God?"

"Dammit Aaron! You know that's why I'm mad at God!" Then Jacob started trailing off, "Or at least I was . . . until last night . . . I'm not sure what . . ."

"Okay . . . okay . . . let's get back to your conversation with Eli. We'll get back to the other issue later."

Jacob had to regather his thoughts, and then continued, "Well, I was telling Grandpa about all that was going on and when I mentioned D'Angelo, he stopped me and asked what his first name was. When I told Grandpa it was Michael, he went off like a bottle rocket and made a beeline down the hill to the house. He said he had something to show me. When I got back to the house, Grandpa was already up in the attic pulling stuff out of a big trunk. Then he handed me a shoebox that was in there."

Aaron turned around facing Jacob, now obviously intent on what he was saying. "So . . . what was in the box?"

"It was Christmas cards with hand written notes that he had received over the years from Elvis."

Aaron almost ran back to the chair next to Jacob's bed and sat down with a stunned expression. "Wait a minute! Are you talkin' 'bout 'hunka . . . hunka . . . burnin' love' Elvis?"

Jacob laughed so hard it made his hip hurt. "Yes Aaron . . . Elvis, the King of 'Rock 'N Roll'. Grandpa met him at a county fair in Alabama way back before Elvis became famous. Grandpa was taken there by a guy who said his name was Michael T Angel. This Angel guy showed up

THE WORDS OF A PROPHITT

at Grandpa's church when Eli was preaching about the sins of 'Rock 'N Roll'. Grandpa said Michael proceeded to tell him that he had the wrong idea about that music and said he wanted Grandpa to meet someone. So, Michael drove Grandpa to the fair. After meeting him, Elvis asked Grandpa to lead a prayer for him and his band before they appeared on stage. Apparently, Elvis never forgot that. Grandpa said after he saw the effect Elvis' music had on the audience, he decided to start using music with his preaching to get the parishioner's attention. That was how his traveling gospel show got started. The weird part of the story is that Grandpa showed me a picture that was taken by a photographer of him standing next to Elvis and Michael. Michael's image didn't develop in the picture. The photographer couldn't explain to Grandpa why it happened."

Aaron sat back in his chair, again tapping his chin with his finger. "Hmmmmmm . . . very interesting. So, what else did you learn on your visit?"

Jacob, beginning to get troubled over Aaron's chin tapping, continued, "Well, then Grandpa showed me pictures of my mother and told me the story about how she and Daddy met at the Woodstock rock concert up in Upstate New York."

"Whoa! Yer parents met at Woodstock? How the heck did that happen?

Jacob had to chuckle at Aaron's enthusiasm. "They were introduced by a guy named Miguel. Apparently, everyone there was calling him Angel."

"Uh . . . Miguel is another translation of . . ."

"Yeah . . . Michael." Jacob hesitated, waiting to see if Aaron tapped his chin again, but instead he continued to sit with a puzzled expression, not moving. Jacob continued, "Well, this Miguel was running a camp serving food and wine to concert goers. My mother was working there and Miguel introduced her to Daddy. Food was running out everywhere else at the venue because the concert was overrun with people, stressing all of the food and water resources. But Miguel had plenty to serve. Later on, he took Daddy and Mom backstage at the concert and he introduced them to Jimi Hendrix.

"Wow! Jimi Hendrix! Did he get any Christmas cards from him?"

Aaron's question struck a nerve and Jacob started laughing hysterically. After regaining his composure, Jacob responded, "No Aaron, not that I saw in the shoebox." Jacob wiped the laughing tears from his eyes and continued, "Anyway, while they were with Hendrix, someone took a picture with one of those Polaroid cameras that would develop in sixty seconds. Mom and Daddy were standing next to Miguel and Jimi Hendrix. After the picture developed Miguel didn't appear in the picture. In fact, Miguel was gone all together. Even the camp he was running disappeared."

Aaron sat back in his chair, still gazing at Jacob. "So, how did your mom and dad get connected from there?"

Jacob laid his head back on the pillow, looking at the ceiling. "That still falls under the weird category. Mom couldn't find the people she came with, so Daddy and his buddies said they would take her home. It ended up she only lived twenty miles away from Grandpa's house."

"NO WAY! Jacob, ya gotta be kiddin' me. That's just insane. Out of a half million people, they meet and they both came from almost the same place? That's incredible!"

Jacob turned his head to look at Aaron. "Yes, it was. It's almost like it was planned . . . if you believe in that sort of thing."

"So, Jacob, is that all?"

"No. There's still a lot more to tell you."

"Really?"

"Yes, really. My mom died after my birth. That's another long story I'll tell you about sometime. But a few years after her death, Dad was having some issues in a church he was preaching at. He took some time off and made a trek back to Woodstock. I guess he was feeling nostalgic about Mom at the time. He told Grandpa that when he was getting close to the town of Woodstock, it was late and he was tired, so he stopped at an old roadside motel to get a room. He was hungry and there was a roadhouse next to the motel, so he went there to see if he could get a sandwich. When he walked in, that Miguel guy who introduced Mom and Daddy was behind the bar."

Aaron was now leaning forward in his chair, with a look of disbelief. "No, that didn't happen."

"That's what Daddy told Grandpa. He said he and Miguel talked all night and Miguel got Daddy drunk on wine. Daddy woke up the next morning in his motel room with a terrible hangover and decided to go back to the roadhouse to eat. Get this . . . when he got there, the place was boarded up. The people at the motel told Daddy the place had been closed for a couple of years."

Aaron got up from his chair and started pacing and looking around the hospital room. "Jacob, are y'all filming me or somethin'? This is just all too incredible! You expect me to believe that story?"

Jacob laughed out loud. "Aaron, I'm only telling you what Grandpa told me. I'm not making all of this up."

Aaron returned to his chair. "So, what did your father do after that?"

"Daddy returned home, resigned from the church, married my step-mother, and moved us all to Nashville where he started working in the music industry. End of story."

Aaron sat quietly for a long time, looking as if he was contemplating something. Eventually he sat back in his chair and spoke, "So, Jacob . . . what happened up on that hill last night?"

Jacob fixed his eyes on the ceiling again, not answering for a few moments. "Oh Aaron, I don't know . . ." Jacob's words trailed off and he became silent again.

"C'mon Jacob! Tell me what you saw last night! I can't help you if you aren't open with me."

Jacob turned to look at his interrogator with fire in his eyes, "ALRIGHT AARON! I'll tell you what I saw last night!" Then immediately the expression on his face relaxed and his words were a lot calmer. "Or at least what I think I saw." Jacob sighed and continued. "I saw a flickering of light on the hill. For some reason it had an unusually strong allure. I decided to finally go check it out. When I reached the clearing, there was an attractive lady sitting in a lawn chair next to a campfire, reading my book."

"The Words of the Prophets?"

"Yes. She was laughing as she was reading it."

Aaron leaned forward. "Your book is funny?"

"Well . . . she seemed to think so. Anyway, she said she was Lucinda and she wanted to publish my next work. I told her I didn't have anything in mind to write. She told me that she had the ideas; she just wanted me to write it. She said she could make me rich and famous and that together we could alter the history of the world."

"Man! That lady sounded awful sure of herself."

"That's for sure. Aaron, you wouldn't believe what she did. She had me way up in the air looking over North America, or at least it felt like it." Jacob paused to gather his thoughts. "Then I heard another voice, and it was D'Angelo."

"Michael?"

"Yes, Michael D'Angelo."

Aaron returned to tapping his chin. "Hmmmmm. So, what happened next?"

"D'Angelo proceeded to tell me that Lucinda was really Lucifer and that she was there to steal my soul. They started arguing about me and suddenly they both grew into giants in full warrior attire with huge swords, still yelling at each other in an indistinguishable language. That's when I started backing toward my bike, hoping to make an escape."

"Whoa . . . Jacob . . . buddy . . . what had y'all been smokin'?"

"I'm telling you Aaron, I hadn't taken anything. I was totally straight. Anyway, those two were wielding their swords, ready to battle, when the campfire exploded upward into the sky. It startled me and that's when I fell backward over my bike, injuring my hip. Then a booming voice, that rattled the mountains, came out of the fire. It said, "Michael, it is not time."

"Wow . . . it sounds like you almost witnessed Armageddon! What happened next?"

"What happened next was, one of the giants shrank back down to a normal size and it was D'Angelo. He knelt down and surrendered himself to the other giant. Then the other one shrank back down and it was Lucinda. She said that was too easy and she wanted a real fight. Then the voice in the fire boomed again telling Lucifer to leave the mountain; she immediately disappeared. After that, the fire went back to its original size and D'Angelo came over next to me and we discussed some things. During our conversation, he all but admitted that he was an angel, but never really came out and said it. Then he had to go. The next thing I remember is the rescue party showing up. That's everything that happened . . . or what I think happened. I'm just not sure.

Maybe I crashed going into the clearing and that knocked me out and I dreamt all of this. All I know is I caused a lot of trouble for a lot of people." Aaron got up from his chair and returned silently to the window. He stood there for a long-time which made Jacob uncomfortable. The silence was deafening. Jacob finally wasn't able to refrain from speaking any longer. "Aaron! What are you thinking? You're making me crazy."

Aaron turned around and leaned against the ledge of the window. "Jacob, how many times in this conversation has the name Michael come up?"

"I'm not sure. I guess I wasn't counting. Why is that important?"

Aaron returned to his chair next to Jacob's bed. "I'm not sure, but the name keeps coming up. Jacob, have you heard the legend of how Woodlock came to be?"

Jacob, unsure what the conversation had to do with his personal situation, replied, "Well, I was told that Jedediah Woodlock came into this valley, fell in love with it, and decided to start a Bible Seminary here."

"Well, that's part of the story. I tend to be fanatical 'bout this kinda stuff. I spent hours at the University library researchin' the history of Woodlock University. Ole Jedediah kept a diary 'bout his travels in the Colonies. He had a lot of entries 'bout his travels south, preachin' and gainin' followers for his cause. Somethin' that I found really interestin' is that he mentions a French trapper that led him to this valley. That trapper's name was Michel, which is pretty much the same as . . ."

Jacob chimed in, "Michael . . . it's the same as Michael. What's that got to do with anything?"

"Jacob, don't y'all see a pattern here? There was a Michael that brought Woodlock to this valley. Eli met Elvis through

Michael. Yer daddy met your mother and Jimi Hendrix through Miguel, or Michael if you choose. President Upton told you he knew D'Angelo. Now y'all possibly have been face-to-face with Satan and most likely heard the voice of God. Who was there?"

Jacob released a large sigh and replied meekly, "Michael D'Angelo."

Aaron's face and body expressed excited anticipation, waiting for a response from Jacob. After a few moments, Aaron ran out of patience and requested an answer, "What do ya think? Isn't this all a little too coincidental?"

Jacob laid his head back and again stared at the ceiling. "Aaron, I don't understand what all of this has to do with my dilemma. All I want to know is, did last night really happen or is it a figment of my imagination? Just give me your professional opinion."

Aaron, somewhat dejected that Jacob didn't share the same enthusiasm about his theory, got up from his chair and returned to the window. He stood silent for what seemed like a long time and then returned to the chair next to Jacob. "So, y'all want my professional opinion?"

"Yes, please. That's all I ask?"

"Okay . . . here it goes. I have two thoughts 'bout what's goin' on with y'all, and it could go either way in my mind. My first diagnosis is that yer crazier than a loon!"

That struck a nerve with Jacob. He immediately sat up erect, forgetting the pain in his hip. "Oh . . . really? And what the hell is your second opinion about me 'mister professional counselor'?"

Aaron chuckled, knowing he had gotten under Jacob's skin. "My second opinion is that someone's tryin' to get yer attention and y'all have been ignorin' whomever that is. If that's the case, then what you experienced on the hill was real."

Jacob laid his head back on the pillow, feeling the negative results of sitting up too quickly. After remaining quiet and spending time contemplating Aaron's words, he responded, "Okay Rabbi Weiss . . . let's say that last night really happened as I remember. . . how can I ever prove it?"

Aaron got up from the chair and stood motionless for a few seconds, then quietly turned and headed toward the door to leave the room. When he reached the door, he turned back toward Jacob. "As a scholar of the Bible, ya well know God works in mysterious ways. I believe that y'all will receive a sign confirming that what ya experienced actually occurred. It will happen when ya least expect. It could be today, next week, or next month. However, I believe it will happen. So, I suggest ya stay on your toes."

Aaron reached for the door handle. Before he could grab it, the door opened. Sherriff Finch entered and was startled when he saw Aaron standing there. Finch removed his hat exclaiming, "Rabbi."

"Sherriff. Good to see ya again."

"Likewise, Rabbi. Please, let me hold the door for you."

"Thank ya, Sherriff Finch." Aaron then turned back to Jacob, "Shalom my friend. I will see ya soon."

After the door closed, Finch walked over to Jacob's bed. "So, Mister Prophitt, we meet again . . . under better circumstances, I hope. How are you feeling today?"

Jacob looked up at the ceiling, rather than facing Finch, not being sure of why he was there. "I am okay. Just a little sore right now." He then turned his gaze to Finch. "So, Sherriff, what is the reason for your visit?"

Finch pulled out a file folder he had tucked under his arm. Opening the folder, he answered, "Well, its both social and business. I wanted to check in and see how you are doing. Also, I just received the toxicology report and I wanted to share the results with you." Finch became quiet as he silently read the report for the first time. After a few moments, he looked at Jacob. "So, it looks like you were clean as a whistle. No alcohol, no drugs, no nothing. So, let me ask you . . . why were you up on that hill last night?"

Jacob returned his gaze to the ceiling. "I told you last night . . . I saw what I thought was a campfire and I went up to investigate."

"I see. Last night you said you saw someone there next to a campfire. Mister Prophitt . . . Jacob . . . we scoured the area and we couldn't find any sign of anyone else being there besides you. What do you make of that?"

Jacob remained quiet while formulating his answer. "Sherriff Finch, in retrospect, I think maybe I crashed and was knocked unconscious for a time. I must have dreamt that someone else was there while I was out. That is the only reasonable explanation I can come up with."

Finch closed the folder and tucked it back under his arm. "I see. Well I guess that explanation will have to do. I will enter it into my report. Jacob, I highly recommend that if you need to ride your bike on these mountain trails, that you do it with a companion. It's not safe riding alone, there's too much that can go wrong."

Jacob, still staring at the ceiling verbally agreed, "Yes sir, Sherriff Finch. I will keep that in mind from now on."

Finch, sensing sarcasm in Jacob's voice, decided his visit was over. "Okay Mister Prophitt, I will be going now. Have a nice day." Finch walked to the door to leave when he suddenly turned back to Jacob. "Oh, by the way, I almost forgot. Are you a golfer Mister Prophitt?"

Jacob, confused, answered, "No, I'm not. Why do you ask?"

Finch returned to Jacob's bedside. "Well, one of the officers found this on the ground next to your bike." Finch reached into his pocket and pulled out a golf tee and handed it to Jacob. "We figured it must have fallen out or your pocket when you crashed."

"Uh . . . no, it's not mine."

"Okay, why don't you keep it as a souvenir? A little reminder of our adventure. I'll see you around."

Sherriff Finch exited the room leaving Jacob alone with his thoughts. While he was lying there staring at the ceiling, Jacob was rehashing his conversation with Aaron and all the while he was absent-mindedly fidgeting with the golf tee. After a while, with boredom setting in, and for no good reason, Jacob decided to inspect the tee. He rolled it around between his fingers and noticed a logo printed on the side of it. With a closer examination of the golf tee, he was able to discern from the faded printing the words 'Augusta National'. Then, it hit Jacob like a bolt of lightning. Astonished, he loudly exclaimed to the empty room, "YOU *WERE* THERE! IT *REALLY* HAPPENED!"

CHAPTER FOURTEEN

JACOB SAT AT THE DESK in his home office with his crutches nearby, working on instructions for the next class session so Rabbi Weiss could substitute for him. Jacob had decided to forego teaching at least until he could graduate to using a cane. It was Saturday and the children were all at home, busy doing various activities. Rebecca was gone as she had decided to work an extra shift at the hospital. So, it was mostly quiet around the house. Jacob's cell phone rang; glancing at the 'caller ID' he did not recognize the number. Usually Jacob ignored calls which he did not recognize but for some reason, on this occasion, he answered, "Hello, this is Jacob."

"Hello . . . Jacob?"

"Yes, this is Jacob Prophitt."

"Jacob . . . it's Jules . . . Jules Kelly . . . Eli's neighbor."

"Oh . . . hi Jules. What can I . . .?"

"Jacob . . . I'm so sorry." And then she began crying. "Jacob . . . Eli passed today. I'm so sorry to have to call you and tell you this." Then Jules began sobbing even harder.

Jacob, feeling like he had just been stabbed in the heart, stayed silent. Then, after regaining his emotions, he managed to respond, "Jules . . . calm down . . . it's alright. What happened?"

Jules continued sobbing on the phone. Finally, able to talk, she continued, "Oh Jacob . . . this is such a terrible day. I watched Eli go up the hill to 'the point' this morning. I have always kept a close watch to make sure he returned to the house. He would usually stay up there for a couple of hours. But today . . ." Then Jules broke down again.

"Jules . . . I know this is hard. Please . . . continue."

"Jacob . . . he didn't come back down to the house and I got worried. I called my husband and he told me to call the Sherriff's office and get someone to check on Eli. So, I did. They sent an officer and he brought some paramedics with him. I showed them the way up the hill and we all entered the clearing together."

Then Jules started sobbing again. Jacob sat patiently, stunned by their conversation. After a time, it sounded to Jacob like she had calmed down and he quietly asked, "Jules . . . are you alright?"

"Yes . . . I'll be okay. It's just so sudden and shocking. Eli was so active. I just can't believe he's gone."

Jacob felt another stab of pain to his inner core, agreeing with Jules' sentiments. Trying to keep his emotions under control for Jules' sake, he calmly prodded her to continue. "Jules, please go on."

Jules, now a little calmer replied, "Well . . . we entered the clearing and we saw Eli just sitting there with his walking stick in his hand. Then we saw that damn rattlesnake coiled up near his feet, with his rattle going a mile a minute, looking right at us."

Jacob interrupted, "Jules . . . do you think it was Beauregard?"

"I don't know Jacob. I guess. I think that's a stupid name for a snake, I don't know why Eli had to give that rattlesnake a name. Anyway, the officer pulled out his gun but was afraid to shoot at it because it was so close to Eli. But that thing suddenly stopped rattling and just uncoiled itself and slithered off into the woods."

"Jules! Was Grandpa bitten by the snake?"

"No . . . when we got to Eli, he was already gone. There wasn't anything the paramedics could do. They checked him over and didn't find any signs of a snakebite. They think he died of natural causes, possibly his heart." Then Jules became silent for a moment. "Jacob, you know the crazy thing? It almost seemed like that stupid snake was guarding Eli's body. Eli was sitting there holding the stick, and he had the most serene look on his face . . . almost like he was smiling." Then Jules broke down again sobbing uncontrollably.

Jacob, doing everything in his power to keep from losing it himself, took in a deep breath before speaking to Jules. "Okay Jules . . . I am going to let you go so you can get some rest. I have to take care of some arrangements."

"Oh, Jacob . . . I almost forgot . . . the County Coroner wants you to contact him and give him instructions on what to do with Eli. He gave me his number and I wrote it down. It's here somewhere . . ."

"Jules . . . when you find it, just text it to me. I'll call him when I get the number. If you could make sure the house is secure until we get there, that would be very helpful."

Jules replied, now sounding more composed, "I will absolutely do that for you Jacob. Let me know if there is anything else that I can do for you and your family. Anything . . . just ask!"

"Thank you, Jules . . . I appreciate your help. I will talk with you soon." Jacob ended the call and sat back in his chair, staring out the window of his office. He wasn't really looking at anything, just staring. The thought of never seeing his grandfather again was just beginning to sink in, and it was heartbreaking. After a long time of holding back tears and clearing his mind, Jacob was jarred back to reality by his phone buzzing, indicating he had received a text. The message he received was from Jules; it was the phone number for the Coroner. Deciding it was time to act, Jacob took a deep breath, trying to sound as normal as possible, and asked loudly, "ARE ANY OF YOU GIRLS NEARBY?"

Within a second, he heard his second oldest, Ruth, reply, "I'm here in the kitchen Daddy! What do you need?"

"Come here please. I need you to do something for me."

Ruth bounded into the office with an excited look of anticipation, eager to help. "What do you want me to do Daddy?"

"Ruth, I need you to go out in the garage and lift up the tarp on the back end of Lizzy and open up the boot. There's a box in there that I need. Can you do that for me?"

"Oh, yeah! I'll be right back!" Ruth ran out of the office and Jacob could hear her as she tore down the hallway, through the kitchen, and out the back with the screen door loudly slamming closed. Jacob had to chuckle at her exuberance. It didn't seem like any time at all until he heard the screen door open and the sound of footsteps coming back toward his office. Ruth entered with a look of accomplishment gingerly carrying the box. "Here it is Daddy!" She carried it around the desk and stood next to Jacob as she set it on the desk in front of him.

Jacob reached around her waist and pulled her close, giving her a peck on the cheek. "Thanks, sweetie. That was very helpful."

Ruth continued to stand next to Jacob, still with an excited look of anticipation. "Can I do anything else for you Daddy?"

THE WORDS OF A PROPHITT

Jacob had to gulp, still restraining his emotions. He kissed her on the cheek again, "No, not right now, but I will call you again if I need anything else. Okay?"

Ruth, in return, kissed Jacob on the cheek, and with a beaming smile left the office, "Okay Daddy! I'm right out here in the kitchen. Just yell!"

Jacob was now alone, staring at the one thing he had dreaded the most . . . the 'box of death'. His mind was telling him to open the box, but his arms would not move . . . almost like he was experiencing paralysis. In his mind, it was almost as if the box was the portal to the end. Finally, after several minutes, his practical side overcame his emotional side and he reached to open the box. Once the lid was lifted off, Jacob found a stack of letters bound together with an elastic band. On top of the stack was a twenty-dollar bill with a post-it-note labeling the money as postage. Jacob smiled to himself thinking about how Grandpa Eli always thought of everything. Removing the elastic band, Jacob sifted through the stack, noticing that Eli had addressed an envelope with a letter to his father, David, and to each of Jacob's sisters. At the bottom of the stack was an envelope with Jacob's name on it; however, it was not addressed. Jacob took a deep breath and then tore open the envelope, finding a hand-written note saying: *My dear Jacob, if you are reading this letter, I have now gone to be with your Grandma Sarah. I have written letters to everyone in your family, and I want those sent out as soon as you hear of my demise. I want you to know that I love you very much and I am proud of whom you have become. I do pray that someday you are able to accept the truth about God . . . that He does exist. I have prayed daily that He blesses you and keeps you and your family safe. My dear grandson, it is my last wish that you and your sisters can all come together as a family. Also, I pray that you will find it in your heart to accept Vicki as your mother here on earth. She has made your father happy and I think she deserves your respect and love. I know you will do the right thing. In this box you will find all of the documents and instructions for what you need to do now that I am gone. I ask that you adhere closely to my wishes. God speed Jacob. This is goodbye, for now.*

Jacob had tears welling up in his eyes and he had a feeling of overwhelming loneliness. The realization that Eli was really gone was hitting him square in the face, and there was nothing he could do to change it. Suddenly, the one thing that Jacob had been avoiding because he felt it would be a sign of weakness happened, the flood gates opened and he cried out loud, holding his face in his hands. After what seemed like hours to Jacob, he calmed himself, grateful that none of his children had seen him break down. He wiped away the tears from his eyes, hoping he wasn't too red-eyed, and called out to Ruth. She again bounded into the office, obviously excited to be helpful again, when she stopped in her tracks, looking at Jacob.

"Daddy, are you okay?"

"Yes . . . I'm fine."

Ruth had a suspicious look on her face. "Are you sure? It looks like you were crying."

"Yes, Ruth, I'm fine. I'm just a little sad about some bad news. We will all talk about it when your Mother gets home. Where's your big sister?"

"She's upstairs reading."

"Would you please go up and get her. I need for you two to run an errand for me."

The excitement returned to Ruth's demeanor. She turned toward the stairway and yelled, "BETHANY! COME DOWN HERE! DADDY NEEDS US TO DO SOMETHING!"

Jacob started laughing, "I asked you to go up and get her . . . not yell up at her."

Ruth, with a sheepish look, replied, "Sorry Daddy."

Bethany, quietly descended the stairs and entered the office. "Hi Daddy, what do . . ."? She also immediately noticed Jacob's red eyes and asked, "Daddy, are you okay?"

"Yes Bethany, I'm fine."

"You look like you have been crying."

"Bethany, I'm fine. I just got some sad news. We will discuss it later. Right now, I need for you and Ruth to get your bikes out and take these letters over to the post office. Here's a twenty-dollar bill to pay for the postage. That's way more money than you to need for stamps, so why don't the two of you stop at the ice-cream stand on the way back and get a treat?"

Bethany, with a suspicious look, responded, "Sure Daddy. Are you sure you are okay?"

"Yes, Bethany, I'm fine. Just do as I ask please."

Bethany, still reluctant, without knowing what was wrong, finally relented. "C'mon Ruth, let's do what Daddy asked. We'll be back in a little bit."

"Okay, you girls be careful crossing the streets. Have fun."

Jacob listened as the two girls quietly left the house. Once he was certain they were gone, he picked up his phone and hit speed dial. After two rings, a familiar voice answered, "Hi Jacob. This is a surprise . . . good to hear from you."

"Uh . . . Daddy . . . I'm afraid you won't be happy to hear from me today."

"Jacob, what's wrong?"

"Uh . . . Daddy . . . it's Grandpa. Daddy . . . he passed this morning."

There was nothing but silence on the other end of the conversation. After a few moments, Jacob finally got a response. "So . . . what happened?"

"We aren't sure yet. The paramedics think it was natural causes, maybe his heart. I have to call the Coroner and make the arrangements for his body. I think we should forgo any autopsies and just have his body sent to the funeral home. He has given me a list of his last wishes and instructions, so I will work on those this afternoon."

David Prophitt was quiet for a short time, as if he was pondering Jacob's comments, "I agree Jacob. I don't think an autopsy would answer anything, after all he was up there in years. Anyway, the last couple of times we spoke, he sounded like he was ready to go home to your Grandma Sarah. I'm sure he's in a happier place now." Jacob felt another surge of tears welling up as his father spoke. Unable to respond for a moment, and being silent, David became concerned and reached out to his son. "Jacob . . . are you alright?"

"Uh . . . yeah . . . I . . . just . . . can't believe this. I can't believe he's gone." And then suddenly the tears began flowing and Jacob couldn't hold back anymore, sobbing loudly into his father's ear.

As he was crying uncontrollably, Jacob heard his father also crying and responding to Jacob, "Let it out Jacob! You have always held in your emotions! Let it out so you'll feel better!" After almost five minutes of crying by both men, they began to regain their composure. David was the first to speak. "Jacob, are you okay?"

"Uh . . . sure Daddy. I'm better now. I'm sorry for breaking down like that. That was so childish."

"There's nothing childish about crying Jacob. You sometimes have to let it out or it will eat you up inside." David chuckled a little, "You had to be the most defiant little poop

THE WORDS OF A PROPHITT

I had ever seen when you were a kid. No matter what the punishment when you were bad, even when I would spank you, you absolutely weren't going to cry. I don't know where you got that from."

"Yeah . . . Daddy . . . about that . . . I want to apologize for the way I acted when I was at home with you and Vicki. Before you sent me to live with Grandpa, I wasn't being fair to either one of you. I don't know where my head was at then."

David didn't answer for a few moments, and then finally replied, "Jacob . . . my son . . . I believe there is enough blame to go around for what was wrong in our family, so don't bear the weight of this solely on your shoulders. There are a lot of things that could have been handled differently, mostly by me. I would ask that you try to be nicer to Vicki in the future. She is your step-mother; she did help raise you."

"You're right Daddy, she does deserve to be appreciated and I promise to do better. I will apologize to her face-to-face at the funeral when we are all together."

"That would be very nice Jacob." Then there was an awkward silence between the two. "I understand that you visited your Grandfather recently. Daddy said that the two of you had quite the discussions."

Jacob was taken back as Eli had asked him to not say anything to David about their conversations. "Uh . . . yes . . . we did talk about a lot of things."

"I understand that Grandpa Eli pretty much told you everything about your mother and me . . . how we met, the circumstances around your birth and her death and how Vicki became your step-mother . . ."

Jacob was getting uncomfortable with the direction the conversation was going, not knowing how much Eli had shared with David. "Yes, he told me a lot about Mom. I even heard her recorded voice from some tapes he had in the attic."

"Well . . . I'm glad he told you everything. This should have been out in the open from day one. I thought I was protecting Vicki by keeping quiet and not sharing the past, but all I really did was hurt the family. I hope everyone can forgive me . . . especially you Jacob."

"Daddy, I don't think you need forgiveness. You were doing what you thought was right. Hopefully we can all move past this and come together. The discussions with Grandpa gave me a new perspective on some things that have been going on in my life. The last few weeks have been really weird."

David laughed at Jacob's comment. "Weird to say the least! I hear you have been doing some crazy stuff . . . like riding a bicycle up the mountain in the dark."

"You've been talking with Rebecca, haven't you?"

"Yes. She's worried about you. She thinks you are stressing out over something."

Jacob was hesitant to speak any further, afraid the conversation would get too deep with his father. After profoundly thinking it through, he continued, "To be clear, it was daylight when I rode up the mountain trail. Yes . . . I have been stressing out. Here I am, a professor at a Christian University, and I had been questioning the existence of a God and I am supposed to be teaching the 'Word of God' for people to preach about . . ."

David interrupted, "Because of Ezekiel."

Jacob, somewhat taken surprised by David's response, answered, "Yes . . . exactly!"

"Just as I did when your mother died."

Jacob was now stunned. "You questioned your faith? I didn't know that."

THE WORDS OF A PROPHITT

"Of course, Jacob. How could I believe in a God that would take the life of my soulmate and the mother of my son? That was not what God was supposed to do. And then, when the hypocrites in the church where I was ministering were making things difficult between Vicki and me, it was the last straw. I was ready to become a full-blown non-believer!"

"So, Daddy... what changed? You obviously still believe. You are producing Christian music and I heard through the grapevine that you have been doing some preaching again lately."

"Well Jacob . . . a long time ago I met up with an old friend at a roadhouse close to Woodstock. He served me too much Communion and showed me the light. I'm certain that your Grandfather shared that story with you."

"He did, but he didn't tell me what happened."

"Daddy couldn't tell you that part . . . I never shared that with him. You are the first person I have ever told this to." David hesitated for a moment, then continued, "Now . . . I understand you have a Michael in your life. How's that working for you?"

Jacob began laughing after that question. David began laughing also, but wasn't sure why. "What's so funny?"

"Grandpa made me swear that I would never let you know that he told me all of this. I'm certain that he made you swear the same thing!"

David, now knowing why Jacob was laughing, responded, "Yes, he did! I think Eli was becoming a sly ole' bird at his advanced age." David laughed a little more and then returned to the subject at hand, "So, tell me about this Michael."

Jacob quickly retorted, "He's rude, crude, and socially inept! He has embarrassed me in front of my colleagues and the public. He thinks he's funny, but he's not. He won't call me by my proper name. He will only address me as 'Doc'."

"When you had your accident up on the mountain the other night, was Michael there?"

"Uh . . . yes he was . . . or I think he was."

"You 'think' he was?"

"Yes, Daddy, I think he was. It's also possible that I was in the presence of God. I may have heard his voice."

"Why? Aren't you convinced?"

"I don't know Daddy! I have pretty strong proof that it all happened, but I'm still not one hundred percent convinced in my own mind. Let me ask you a question. If you are so convinced that God exists, why haven't you ever told me so?"

"I told you many times when you were young, but you were always the skeptic. You were always so angry. Sometimes, people such as yourself, have to have proof to believe. It's not enough for many to hear someone testify the 'Truth'. They have to see it firsthand. It sounds to me like you are almost there. You just need that last little push off the edge."

"You may be right Daddy. We'll see how things turn out. I do need a favor from you though, if you don't mind."

"Sure Son, what do you need?"

"Would you please contact everyone in the family and let them know about Grandpa? I need to get busy with arrangements and it would help to know when everyone can get to Somerset."

"I will certainly do that Jacob. I will get their schedules and let you know as soon as I hear."

"Thanks Daddy . . . I love you."

There was a long, stunned hesitation on the other end of the call. "I love you too Son."

CHAPTER 15

It was Friday, and the Prophitt family was on the road to Somerset for Eli's funeral. The van was loaded down with all of the necessary provisions for a two-day trip with a family of eight. Rebecca had arranged for all of the children to leave school early so the family could make it to the funeral home by late afternoon for the public visitation. After being on the road for a couple of hours, all of the children had settled into wearing their headphones and were either listening to music, reading, or playing games, so the van was quiet, other than the whining of the tires over the ever-changing road surfaces.

Jacob was quietly riding in the passenger seat. Jacob usually drove, but Rebecca had refused to let him drive while he needed to use crutches to get around. Being able to watch the scenery rather than the road on the trip to Somerset was something foreign to him. As they traveled along, Jacob was recalling his childhood days when he stayed with his grandparents. During that time, he learned about woodworking from his Grandpa Eli. A smile came to his face recalling the times he would sit on the front porch whittling on wood he and his grandfather had picked up in the forest around the house. Eli had taught Jacob how to use a pocket knife and the art if honing it to a keenly sharp edge so it would carve wood like cutting butter. While whittling, they would talk about life and religion, especially religion, while sipping on the sweet tea that Grandma Sarah would brew up for them to have after a hard day of working in the yard.

Soon all of the pleasant thoughts Jacob was enjoying turned to dread as the realization of why they were traveling to Somerset returned. Rebecca had been watching Jacob out of the corner of her eye trying to read his thoughts. "Honey . . . are you okay?"

The question startled Jacob. "Huh? Uh . . . yeah . . . I'm alright. Why do you ask?"

"I was sort of watching you and you suddenly started frowning. What were you thinking about?"

Jacob wasn't really sure what he was thinking when his expression changed, other than dread.

"Oh . . . I guess after a few moments of pleasant memories of my youth, the dread over this trip returned to me."

Rebecca continued to look straight ahead at the road, asking, "So, what are you dreading the most?"

Jacob had to ponder that question for a few moments as there were several different things that he was dreading all at the same time. Finally, he responded, "I think the biggest dread I have is coming face-to-face with my family. I haven't even spoken with most of my sisters literally for years. I don't even know them anymore. There will be aunts, uncles, brothers-in-law, nieces, nephews and hard telling who else that I haven't ever met or even knew of. I don't know what the atmosphere is going to be like. There was never a lot of joy in our family being together, other than with Jennifer. She's the only one I got along with and enjoyed being around. So, there's a lot of unknowns and I'm really feeling uncomfortable. I'm afraid we'll be walking into a potential hornet's nest."

THE WORDS OF A PROPHITT

Rebecca laughed. "One sure thing about you Jacob is you are the consummate pessimist. Don't you think that after all these years that things might lighten up, especially when all of you are coming together at a funeral for your grandfather? I know things were kind of cool between all of you at Sarah's funeral, but maybe things have changed."

"Yeah, well you are the ultimate optimist. Grandpa Eli explained to me when I visited him that my older sisters blame me for Mom's death and that's why they don't like me. That's something that will be hard to overcome. The only reason Jennifer doesn't hate me is that she was too young to remember much about our mother, and we were usually together when we were growing up. Daddy never shared what really happened with my sisters, so they don't know the whole story."

"Well, Jacob . . . we'll just have to wait and see."

"Yeah . . . we'll see."

The conversation ended there and not much more was said between Jacob and Rebecca for the rest of the trip. Once they reached Somerset, Jacob found the directions to where they needed to go on his cell phone. After traveling down a few more streets, they finally came upon a huge Victorian style home that had been converted to a funeral parlor. Jacob and Rebecca were stunned by the amount of people who were standing in a line, reaching far down the street to the end of the block. Obviously, they were waiting to enter the funeral home to pay their respects. The parking lots and the street parking were all filled up. Finally, a police officer who was directing traffic came up to the van, so they stopped.

"Hi folks. I'm sorry but everything is filled up. There's more parking over on the next block."

Rebecca asked, "Officer, are you sure there isn't anything closer? This is Eli Prophitt's grandson. He's on crutches."

"Oh . . . I'm sorry ma'am! There's a reserved parking spot for you at the family entrance. Pull on around the side of the building and I will move the safety cone blocking the space."

"Thank you, officer." Rebecca pulled in behind the policeman, following him as he walked around to the parking space. While she was creeping along, she commented, "Wow! Can you believe the number of people that are here?"

Wide eyed, Jacob answered, "No, I don't believe this! I had no idea he knew this many people in Somerset. This is going to take all night."

Once Rebecca parked the van, everyone piled out and entered the building through the side entrance. Jacob led the way on crutches. A short distance down a hallway, he found a door that had a 'family lounge' sign on it. Not sure what to expect, he gingerly pushed the door open and peeked in. Much to Jacob's relief, the first person he saw was his sister Jennifer. Knowing she would be wound up like an eight-day clock, Jacob braced himself and then quietly said, "Hi Sis. We're here.

Jennifer turned to look and when she saw Jacob, she exploded, "OH MY GOD! OH MY GOD! YOU'RE FINALLY HERE!" She ran across the room and wrapped her arms around Jacob's neck, almost knocking him over. "I've been waiting all afternoon to see you . . . you're on crutches, what's wrong . . . it's so good to see you, it's been so long . . . you have a ponytail. What's with that Mister Doctorate big-shot?" Jennifer continued without seeming to take a breath . . . "Oh . . . hi Rebecca! You look as beautiful as ever. How do you stay so fit? Oh . . . the girls are all getting so big, and beautiful. Bethany and Ruth look like they were carved out of their mother's butt. And Zeke . . . you're getting so big. I bet he doesn't remember me. He was just a little baby the last time I saw him . . . Jacob, why are you on crutches? What did you do to yourself?"

Jacob gingerly placed his hand over her mouth. "Hi Jennifer. It's really nice to see you too. We will all be happy to answer all of your questions while we are together. So, take a breath and let us all freshen up after the long drive we just had and then we will start catching up." Jacob slowly removed his hand from her mouth and she just grinned and nodded her head in agreement. "Okay, now tell us what we need to know about this place."

Jennifer took a deep breath to stay calm, "Well, this is the family lounge where we can take a break. The main room is down at the end of the hall. That's where the viewing is. And . . . this is really cool . . . there is a game room across the hall so the kids can stay busy and not have to deal with all this stuff. My two are over there now if you want your kids to go over there."

Rebecca chimed in, "I think that's a great idea. Jacob you better get out there with the rest of the family. Kids, lets go see your cousins."

Jacob watched everyone leave and decided that he had better do what Rebecca suggested. Using his crutches, he slowly made his way to the main hall. When he entered, he immediately saw his father standing nearest to the casket in the receiving line. Jacob made his way close enough to speak with him. "Hi Daddy. We made it."

David turned and smiled. "Well, you *are* finally here. Did you have a good trip?"

"Sure. Rebecca drove so I got to sightsee."

"Good. Why don't you get between me and Robin? I had the funeral director bring out a stool for you to use. I thought it would be easier than trying to stand on your bum leg."

While David pulled up the stool, Jacob exclaimed, "Man! I can't believe how many people are here. Grandpa Eli must have been well known in town."

David grinned at his son. "This isn't just people from Somerset. There are many people from out-of-town. A lot of them are people Eli brought to God with his gospel shows. Word traveled fast when he passed."

Jacob shook his head in wonder of the humanity. He settled at his place next to his oldest sister, Robin. When she was done talking with a couple in line, she turned to Jacob. "Well, hello Jacob. Long-time-no-see. You're looking very fit, except for those crutches . . . and what is going on with that pony tail thing you have going on there?"

"Hello Robin. It's nice to see you also. It has been a long time."

"Did your family come with you?"

"Yes ma'am, the entire tribe came along."

"Oh good. That means I get to finally meet that lovely wife of yours. It's Rebecca isn't it?"

"Yes . . . it is."

"Great! We'll have a lot to talk about I am sure." Then Robin turned back to the people in line to view Eli.

Jacob was a bit taken back by how pleasant Robin was being to him; however, he didn't have much time to focus on that because of people wanting to give their condolences. The line seemed to be never-ending.

As the evening wore on, the lineup of family would rotate to give everyone a break. Eventually Jacob was situated next to each of his remaining sisters . . . Amie, Jackie, and Angela. And much to his surprise, each one was nicer to him than he ever remembered them being before.

After a couple of hours of meeting people, Jacob decided to move out of the reception line and go to the lounge to rest his hip. Just as he was getting his crutches under his shoulders, he looked up and thought he saw a very familiar face out in the throng of people standing around and visiting in the room. Taking a second look, he was convinced it was D'Angelo standing and talking with someone, having a hearty laugh with whomever he was conversing with. Jacob began to make his way through the crowd, in hopes of catching up with him. As he got closer, Jacob attempted to get his attention by talking over the crowd without actually yelling, "Mister D'Angelo! Michael! I need to talk with you!" The room was packed and it was hard for Jacob to maneuver around on crutches. Trying his best to be polite, he attempted every move he could think of to plow his way through the crowd to get closer to D'Angelo. Every time he thought he was making progress, D'Angelo was further away. He finally made his way to the edge of the room and saw D'Angelo exit down a corridor. Jacob, sure that he finally was going to catch him, made his way to the corridor and saw an exit sign over the door at the end. Jacob went through the door and ended up on what appeared to be a loading dock. It was on the back of the building and near a dark street. Looking both ways, Jacob didn't see D'Angelo anywhere. Then, suddenly, a set of headlights came around the building onto the street. It was a familiar long black Mercedes and it slowed down to a crawl as the driver side window went down. D'Angelo yelled out, "Sorry Doc, we have an early tee time at Augusta National. We'll have to drive all night to make it. Can't chat right now. See ya!" Then the car sped up and D'Angelo waved from the driver side window as Jacob watched him pull away. As the car passed under a street light, Jacob saw another arm waving from the passenger side window. Jacob wondered to himself, "Who the heck would be riding around with, and even wanting to golf, with D'Angelo?"

Feeling dejected at missing him, Jacob went back in the funeral home. Once inside, he noticed that the crowd was thinning out and the end of the line was now inside the entrance. He made his way through the room and down the hall to the lounge. When he entered the only person there was Vicki. She was sitting on an overstuffed sofa leafing through a magazine, and when she noticed Jacob she looked up and smiled without saying anything. Jacob made his way over and sat down next to her. He sat motionless for a few moments and then worked up the nerve to speak. "Vicki . . . uh . . . we need to talk."

Vicki laid the magazine on the lamp table next to her and turned toward Jacob with a suspicious expression, "Okay . . . let's talk."

Clearing his throat, Jacob spoke before he could chicken out. "Vicki . . . I owe you a huge apology." Vicki's expression immediately changed from suspicion to amazement. She wasn't expecting those words to come out of Jacob's mouth. "I have been a total jerk to you for as long as I can remember. I don't know why, but I was mad and I really don't know why I was that way, other than maybe I didn't feel like I had a mother. That wasn't fair to you. You inherited this family under difficult circumstances and you have always been there for all of us kids, and especially for Daddy." Tears started welling up in Vicki's eyes as Jacob was speaking. "I have recently concluded that I may not have had my mother, but I did have a mom, and that was you. I didn't appreciate that. I hope you can forgive me."

Vicki broke down and began sobbing loudly as she moved closer to Jacob and wrapped her arms around his neck pulling him close to her. Jacob responded by giving her a big hug and holding her while she was crying. Suddenly the door to the lounge opened and Rebecca entered, seeing Vicki and

Jacob in an embrace. She went over and sat next to Vicki, asking, "Is everything alright?"

Vicki started laughing and pulled back from Jacob. "Oh, Jacob, I'm leaking on your shirt. I hope I didn't get mascara on it." Then she turned to Rebecca. "Oh, yes dear! Everything is fine. Your husband just made me the happiest step-mom in the world. He spoke the words I have been dreaming of hearing for years."

Rebecca looked at Jacob, asking, "Who are you and what have you done with my husband?"

Again, the lounge door opened. David stepped in and announced, "Everyone is gone from the main hall. Let's all go out and say our final goodbyes to Daddy. We won't have time in the morning before the graveside service." Rebecca left and went across the hall to get the children, Vicki went out to retrieve other family members. As David and Jacob made their way toward the main hall, David asked, "Are you coming out to Daddy's house tonight?"

"Yeah, we were planning on it. We figured there was enough room for all of us."

"Good! I think everyone else got rooms at the hotels. We'll see you there."

David walked on ahead to direct everyone for the small private service he had planned. All of the aunts, uncles, sisters, in-laws and children gathered and stood quietly as David spoke a few words about his father and then finished with a prayer. Before closing, he added, "The graveside service will be at ten in the morning at the graveyard. Jules Kelly, Eli's neighbor and other people that live in Daddy's neighborhood are putting together a feast for all of us to enjoy after the funeral and they ask that you all attend. I also ask that you attend. We need to come together and break bread as a family and remember Eli and Sarah. Now, let's all say our last goodbyes and go and get some rest. Good night."

Every person in the room quietly lined up to pass by the casket that held Eli's lifeless body. Everyone urged Jacob and his family to go first since it was late and they had young children and Jacob was on crutches. Jacob's family gathered at the casket momentarily saying their final goodbyes. When they were finished, Jacob and Rebecca led their children toward the exit, making their way to the van for the trip to Grandpa Eli's house.

After a very quiet ride from the funeral home, Jacob and his family pulled into the driveway at Eli's, finding that all of the exterior and interior lights at the house had been turned on making it safer to enter. Jacob assumed that it was the handywork of Jules Kelley. Once the van had been unloaded and everyone was inside, Rebecca proceeded to get the children ready for bed.

After a short time, David and Vicki arrived. When David entered the house, he sought out Jacob. "Come here! I want to show you something!" Jacob followed his father into Eli's office and instantly noticed that David had carried down a bunch of the boxes from the attic that held pictures. "I thought it would be fun to let everyone see these pictures, kind of giving everyone a little history of our family. I know that Daddy shared some of these pictures with you when you visited so I want you to see something." David reached into one of the shoe boxes and pulled out a picture and handed it to Jacob.

Looking at the picture, Jacob immediately recognized it as the photo that was shot with Eli and Elvis Presley posing with the band. After closer examination, Jacob looked at his father and exclaimed, "No Way! That's not possible!" Jacob looked at the photo again to confirm what he was seeing.

"Is that the Michael T Angel guy standing next to Elvis who introduced Elvis to Grandpa?"

With astonishment, David shook his head affirming Jacob's question. "Yeah . . . I guess so. He wasn't in the picture when Daddy showed it to me before. But, that's not all. Let me show you this." David reached into another box of pictures and handed Jacob another photo.

"Jacob looked at it and then looked up at his father. "Is that Miguel standing next to you and Mom with Hendrix?"

"Yes, it is! I was there when the photo was developed, and he didn't show up in it then. In fact, he completely disappeared from the area shortly after that photo was taken. I don't know what's going on."

"You've got to be kidding me!" Jacob continued staring at the picture in total shock. "Man! I feel like I'm living in the 'Twilight Zone'!

David responded with a disturbed laugh. "Yeah . . . I know what you mean. So . . . uh . . . let me ask you a question."

Jacob, still staring at both photos, looked up at David. "Sure. Anything."

David hesitated for a moment, and then took a deep breath. "So, did you happen to see that D'Angelo guy you told me about at the funeral home?"

Jacob, looking puzzled, felt blindsided by his father's question. "Uh . . . yeah . . . I did. How did you know?"

"I saw you making your way through the crowd in a hurry, so I figured you were after someone. I thought maybe it was him."

"It was D'Angelo, but I wasn't able to talk to him. He went out a back door, and I followed, but he was already gone. Then he drove by in his car and yelled that he had an early tee time and couldn't chat. Then he drove off. He had someone with him, but it was dark and I couldn't see who it was."

David remained quiet for a short time, and then spoke, "I have to confess, I saw someone in the crowd that I tried to catch up to."

Jacob had returned to staring at the photos. Things at this point had gotten so strange that he looked up from the pictures and nonchalantly asked, "Miguel?"

"Yes, I'm sure it was him. I followed him and he went into the men's room. I waited around to talk with him, but he was in there forever. Finally, I opened the door and he was gone. There wasn't anyone in there. I know I saw him go in."

Jacob returned to examining the photos and replied, "Doesn't surprise me."

David laughed at Jacob's comment. "Yeah, I have to admit I'm not surprised either." Letting out a huge sigh, David announced, "You know what? I'm very tired. I give up, I'm going to bed. Goodnight Son. Sleep well"

"Goodnight Daddy. See you in the morning."

David left the office and Jacob lingered, re-examining the photos. Deciding to also give it up, he turned out the lamp on the desk and headed for bed. When he finally made it up the stairs to the bedroom, everyone was sleeping soundly. Jacob went to the bathroom, brushed his teeth, and then made his way back to the bedroom and quietly got into bed next to Rebecca. Jacob lay quietly, listening to all of the breathing from his wife and children while staring at the ceiling in the darkness, thinking about the photographs, D'Angelo and Miguel and wondering what the next day was going to bring. The windows were open and he could hear the wind rustling through the dry fall leaves. Then, he heard the warning sound of a rattlesnake. He smiled to himself, thinking it strange that the sound of a rattlesnake could be so comforting. That was the last thought he had before going to sleep.

CHAPTER 16

SATURDAY MORNING, JACOB WAS AWAKENED when Rebecca rolled out of bed. She started rousing the children, prodding them to get up so they could get their day started. The early morning quiet soon turned into total chaos with six children and four adults attempting to get bathed or showered, dressed, and ready to go all at once. Rebecca and Vicki went into the kitchen to put together a quick breakfast so everyone wouldn't have to go to the graveside service on empty stomachs. Before long, everyone was ready to get on the way to the graveyard. As Jacob was getting into the van, a car pulled into the driveway. It was Eli's neighbor Jules. She climbed out of her car and waved at Jacob. "Hi Jacob. I ran out of oven space at home. I thought I would put some things in Eli's oven. I hope you don't mind."

Jacob smiled and waved back, not answering. He finished getting into his seat and Rebecca headed the van out of the driveway. After a short time, they arrived at the graveyard. Rebecca pulled the van onto the road that would take them to the gravesite. Once they made it to the site, Jacob observed that the casket had been placed next to Grandma Sarah's grave, and a sizeable crowd had already gathered. The people there were standing around and chatting while waiting for the service to begin. Chairs were set up for the family members close to the where the casket was placed. All other attendees would be standing. Jacob and his family found their seats in the second row from the front as the front row chairs were for David and Jacob's aunts.

It was a beautiful, late fall morning. The sun was out, the temperature was comfortable, even without a jacket. The birds were singing and squirrels were playing in the trees above the gravesite, much to the delight of Ezekiel. At exactly ten o'clock, the minister officiating the service moved in and took his place at the podium. He opened with a prayer for the Prophitt family and guests, and then began his eulogy by telling humorous stories about his personal relationship with Reverend Eli Prophitt and their in-depth discussions about theology. Next, he continued with Eli's biography, talking about Eli's love for his wife, Sarah, and for his family as well as touting his many accomplishments and praising Eli for bringing the blessed 'Word of God' to the masses through his traveling gospel shows. At the end of the eulogy, some former choir members from Eli's gospel show got together and sang his favorite hymn, 'Amazing Grace'. When they finished singing, the minister closed the service with a final prayer, and then it was done. After the service, most of the family members left immediately to go to Eli's house for the impromptu family reunion.

Once arriving at Eli's, Rebecca pulled into the long drive and parked in the yard near the house. Many had already arrived, and there were tables and chairs set up everywhere for the hungry crowd. Jacob found a chair and watched Jules who was still organizing things while other neighbors were still delivering dishes of food. After a time, David and Vicki arrived after finishing up some final burial details. When it appeared that everyone was present, Jules grabbed David and led him to the front porch of the house where Eli had a large dinner bell. David rang the bell to get everyone's attention and Jules yelled out instructions on where to get in line to fill their plates. David then led everyone in prayer. When finished, he said, "Amen . . . let's eat!" Everyone laughed and then headed for the food line.

It turned out to be a pleasant day for everyone. The food was excellent and the company was delightful. There was a lot of laughter, tears, conversations, getting reacquainted, making plans for the future and children playing. Everyone there was greatly entertained by the pictures that David had laid out to be viewed. He personally took a large amount of ribbing over the pictures from his hippy days.

Jacob was sitting and talking with Robin's husband Charles, whom he had never spoken with before, when he was interrupted by his sister Jennifer. "Sorry to barge in, but Daddy wants to see you in Grandpa's office."

Jacob looked up at his sister and queried, "What did I do now?"

"Nothing silly, he needs to see you. He said it's important."

"Okay. Sorry Charles, I'll catch up with you later." Jacob got on his crutches and he followed Jennifer into the house, down the hall, and into the office. When he walked through the door, Jacob saw David was sitting at Eli's desk with the rest of his sisters sitting in a semi-circle around the room. Jacob was confused about what was going on, and questioned, "What is this . . . an inquisition?"

Robin spoke up, answering, "No it's not an inquisition, it's an intervention, over that stupid ponytail and beard you are sporting!" Then everyone in the room broke out in laughter. Jacob, feeling very uncomfortable, took a seat and Jennifer closed the door to the office before sitting next to him. After the laughter died down, Robin continued, "We have been in here having a discussion with Daddy over the letters we girls received from Grandpa Eli. I assume you mailed them to us?"

Jacob, still uncertain about what was going on was reluctant to speak. "Uh . . . yes . . . I did mail them. They were in a box with instructions Grandpa gave me with things to do at the time of his passing."

"Did you read any of them?"

"No, I did not. Why? What's going on?"

Robin looked over at David indicating that he should be the one to speak. Taking the hint, he began, "Well Jacob, those letters that Eli had you send gave a complete explanation to your sisters about the circumstances that led up to your birth, and subsequently your mother's death. He sent me a letter telling me what he had done. So, all of us have been sitting here hashing this all out. So many times, I wanted to tell everyone about what really happened. When I thought I would have the courage to do it, I would chicken out. I really don't know why I couldn't share it with all of you, but I am ashamed of what I have done. I know it has caused a lot of problems between all of you kids. I am truly sorry."

Almost immediately, David broke down crying. Simultaneously, all of Jacob's sisters began crying as well. Jacob just sat there, feeling numb, still not sure about where all of this conversation was going.

Finally, everyone regained their composure and Robin was the first to speak. "Jacob, I for one want to apologize for how I have treated you. I always blamed you for Mom's death. I never knew that she was absolutely determined to give birth to you, no matter the ultimate cost. Of course, you weren't to blame . . . you had no choice in the matter. I, or rather we were wrong to treat you like we did. I hope you can forgive us." Jackie, Amie, and Angela all chimed in agreeing with their older sister. Jennifer simply reached over to her brother and held his hand.

After a long period of silence, and everyone wiping their eyes to dry up their tears, Jacob cleared his throat and spoke. "This is all very overwhelming, I'm not sure what I'm feeling right now. I just found out about Mom a short time ago when I came here to visit with Grandpa Eli. He showed me the pictures of Mom, and he even had some recordings. I actually got to hear her voice for the first time. It was all so surreal. It turns out that it was her voice that has been in my head. She spoke to me right before she passed, and I have been hearing those words over and over again my entire life." Jacob paused in an attempt to keep his composure. "As far as forgiveness, I am asking all of you girls to forgive me. I know I was a rotten brat when I was younger."

Angela blurted out, "You got that right bro!" Everyone in the room broke out in laughter again.

Jacob confessed, "Anyway, I know I made it hard for you to like me, so not all the blame is on you girls. I'm trying my best to be a better person. I've had a lot of anger issues, and then coping with my son's health, it's been really hard on me. Hopefully things are getting better."

Robin stood up and announced, "With the power given to me as an ordained minister, I now pronounce this to be one-big-happy-family. We need a group hug!" Everyone met in the middle of the office and joined in the hug. Finally, everyone broke away from the group hug and began hugging individually. Then ringleader Robin made her next announcement. "Okay girls, you know what we need to do next?" All of the sisters had confused looks, not responding. "We need dirt on little brother, and I know right where to get it."

Angela spoke up, "Yeah ... we need to induct 'Red' into the sisterhood of Prophitt women! I bet she'll fold like an omelet!" All the sisters headed for the door and Jacob heard one of them exclaim as they were heading down the hallway, "I want to be the bad cop this time!"

Jacob looked at his father. David sat down in the office chair and replied, "Well Jacob my son ... I believe Rebecca is in big trouble." Then both men started laughing.

Jacob made his way over to the window to look out and see where everyone was at in the yard. He saw that the sisters had surrounded Rebecca at a picnic table and were already grilling her. "She's in really big trouble."

"Uh ... Jacob, I need to talk with you about something."

Jacob moved away from the window and took a chair across the desk from his father. "Sure, what do you want to talk about?"

"Well, I had an opportunity to talk with your sisters before you came in, and we didn't get back to the subject, but Vicki and I are thinking about selling our house in Nashville and moving here. We've been here for a few days and we really like it. I could even turn part of the barn into a recording studio and work from here. I've been needing some new inspiration, and meditating up on 'the point' might be the right medicine for me to do that at this time. What do you think?"

Jacob didn't hesitate. "I think it would be great! I was worried about how we were going to maintain this place and keep it in the family. Plus, you would be about five hours closer to us and we could visit more often. I'm in ... you have my approval."

"Thanks Jacob. All of your sisters said the same thing. Vicki will be excited when I tell her the news. Now, maybe we need to go out and run interference for Rebecca."

THE WORDS OF A PROPHITT

Both Jacob and David returned to the festivities outside. It appeared that the food was gone and Jules and her friends were busy cleaning up. David had suggested to Jules that he and Vicki would finish cleaning up, but Jules would have nothing to do with that. She was there to do a job, and she was going to finish it. David was surprised at how long everyone was hanging around. Now, being the eldest son in the family, he was taking personal pride in watching everybody getting along and enjoying the visit.

Late in the afternoon, Rebecca broke away from the sisters and sought out Jacob to remind him that they needed to get on the road back to Woodlock, so they could be home before it got too late. Jacob announced out loud that they needed to leave and everyone gathered around him and his family to say goodbye. After another forty-five minutes of goodbyes, hugs, tears and laughter, the van was loaded up and the Prophitts were headed east toward Woodlock, Tennessee.

The drive was very quiet on the way home. The children who weren't asleep had their headphones on, engrossed in whatever they were listening to, so there was no conversation in the back of the van. Rebecca and Jacob had not spoken at all either. Both of them had been deep in their own thoughts the entire time. Finally, Rebecca broke the silence. "So, Mister Prophitt . . . did you expect all of this to happen?"

Jacob looked over at Rebecca, somewhat startled by her voice. "Uh . . . no . . . not even in my wildest dreams. It's almost like 'The Reverend Eli Prophitt' orchestrated the entire event and put the words in everyone's mouths, including mine. This whole thing was absolutely crazy. I'm glad it all happened . . . but it was crazy."

Rebecca nodded her head in agreement. Then, still looking straight ahead focusing on the road, "Your sisters are crazy women. It's a shame you have missed all of that when you were growing up."

"Yeah . . . I know. I do regret that."

Rebecca was silent again for a few more miles. Then she asked, "Have you had time to pay much attention to Zeke this last couple of days?"

"No, not really. I mean I've tried to . . . but this has been a roller coaster. Why do you ask?"

"Well, he's been going a hundred miles-an-hour. When he was playing with his cousins, he was non-stop. He usually 'poops out' quickly. I've tried to give him his medicine, but he refuses. He says it makes him feel yucky. So, I just quit trying. I figure if he gets sick, he'll take it then."

"That is strange. Maybe it's adrenaline, or he's possibly going through one of those periods the doctor told us about when things ease up with the fibrosis for a little while. Hopefully he stays that way. We'll just have to pray that he's better."

Rebecca turned her head to look at Jacob. "PRAY?"

Jacob, staring off in the distance, remarked, "Yes pray . . . Mrs. Prophitt!"

"Really! Who are you and what have you done with my husband?"

CHAPTER 17

It had been two weeks since the funeral. Jacob had now graduated to using a cane and was able to maneuver around much easier than with the crutches. The weather in Woodlock had turned cold and blustery so Jacob had to pull out the long pants and start wearing real shoes. In another eventful occurrence, much to Rebecca's delight, after all of the remarks from his sisters about his ponytail and beard, Jacob got his hair cut short and shaved his beard. Hardly anyone recognized him after that. He looked so young that Rebecca was afraid that people would accuse her of robbing the cradle. Jacob figured he would have to reintroduce himself to his class when he returned, or even show his identification badge to confirm who he was.

On this particular day, Jacob was to make his return to the classroom. Before he was able to go to the University, he and Rebecca had to stop by the hospital for a meeting with their family doctor. Ezekiel had been there five days earlier having his usual scheduled check-up to monitor his health and the progression of the Cystic Fibrosis. The doctor would usually hand Rebecca the updated reports when she was at work, but this time he requested a conference with both parents. Not knowing what to expect, both Jacob and Rebecca were on pins and needles waiting for the meeting.

When they arrived at Doctor Griffin's, his receptionist escorted them to his office, telling them that the doctor would be with them shortly. Jacob was too nervous to sit in a chair, so he was up wandering around the room looking at pictures and diplomas that were hanging on the walls, trying to occupy his mind. Rebecca was sitting, but fidgeting around while playing solitaire on her cell phone, attempting to keep her composure. Finally, the door to the office swung open and Doctor Griffin entered the room. "Reading my diplomas to see if I'm really a doctor Jacob?"

A startled Jacob turned around, red-faced with embarrassment and replied, "Uh . . . no. I was just looking at things you have on the walls."

Doctor Griffin laughed at Jacob's nervousness. "Come and sit down. I have some news for you folks. I'm not quite sure how, or why I have this news, but I do." Then he sat back in his large leather office chair and looked at the both of them, not saying anything. Then he leaned forward and placed his arms on his desk. "I'm sure going to miss seeing the little guy . . .

Suddenly, Jacob and Rebecca simultaneously yelled out, "WHAT?"

Doctor Griffin held up his hand stopping them. "Let me finish . . . I'm going to miss seeing the little guy as much as I used to. Right now, you have yourselves a healthy, almost six-year-old boy."

Rebecca and Jacob looked at each other and then turned back looking at the doctor with stunned looks. After a long silence, Rebecca finally spoke up. "Doctor, what are you trying to tell us?"

"I am trying to tell you that your son is a healthy kid. He has no signs of Cystic Fibrosis in his system. Everyone here at this hospital are flabbergasted on this one. I have checked and rechecked the results of the tests a dozen times. I have communicated with every specialist that I could find to talk with and had them review the results. I have been told that there have been instances where the disease has gone into remission with the use of some experimental drugs, but in this case, Zeke's just plain healthy. I would like to be able to take credit for all of this, but this is the work of a higher power. To me, this is nothing short of a miracle."

Jacob and Rebecca were too astonished to speak or move. They were glued to their chairs staring expressionlessly at Doctor Griffin. Finally, Jacob was able to speak. "So, that's it? We're done here?"

"Well, yes... unless one of you have an ailment of some kind I don't know about. I do suggest that we continue to watch Zeke's health for a while longer, but I honestly do not think he is going to have any more issues other than the usual childhood colds and flu."

All Rebecca could say was, "Wow!"

Doctor Griffin stood up from his chair. "Okay folks, I have patients that are sick and need my attention. If you don't have any other questions, I'm going to go attend to them. You two can stay in here until you comprehend the great news and are able to walk out on your own power. Have a blessed day." Then he picked up some medical files and walked out of the office, leaving the two of them with their thoughts.

Together they sat silently for a long time. Finally, Rebecca spoke up. "Jacob, what happened on that mountain the night you got hurt?"

"I told you the truth that night and you didn't believe me. You thought I was crazy."

"So, you really talked to God?"

"No, I said I was in the presence of God. I heard His voice. He was speaking to D'Angelo and Lucifer." Jacob then looked at his watch. "I have to get to the University for class." Standing up to leave, he grabbed Rebecca's hands and held them tight. "Rebecca, you won't believe everything that has gone on in my life the past few weeks, and all of the stories Grandpa Eli told me. I want to share all of that with you. I promise I will tell you everything. Believe me it will blow your mind." Jacob gave Rebecca a kiss and then headed for the door.

Before he could open the door, Rebecca asked, "So do you believe in God?"

Jacob turned to her with a big smile. "Indubitably!" Then he exited the office.

Jacob crossed the hospital parking lot and climbed into Lizzy. When he arrived at the parking lot at the University, he pulled into a spot close to the front entrance of Peterson Memorial Hall. Making his way using his cane to climb the steps, he opened the heavy glass door and entered the hall. As he began his climb up the stairs to the first floor, Jacob was startled by a familiar voice at the top of the stairs. "GOOD MORNIN' DOCTOR PROPHITT! HOW Y'ALL DOIN' ON THIS BLUSTERY MORNIN'?"

Jacob laughed, remembering when he first met Rabbi Weiss. "Good morning Aaron. I am having a wonderful today. We just received some amazing news and I am one happy professor!"

"Yeah, I just heard. Rebecca already called Mindy. She couldn't contain herself. I guess we're havin' dinner at yer house tonight to celebrate. She said we're havin' Zeke's favorite dish. By the way . . . what is tater-tot casserole?" Aaron laughed as he began descending the stairs.

THE WORDS OF A PROPHITT

Jacob met Aaron on the stairwell halfway up. "Where are you going?"

"I've got stuff ta do. I just stopped in ta see if y'all would actually show up. I've got Christians to convert don't ya know? I don't have time to chit-chat. See ya later." Aaron exited the building, waving his hand over his head as he whisked through the door.

Jacob laughed with amusement at Aaron's comment and then finished climbing the stairs. Once on the main level, he made his way to the classroom. He was still a few minutes early, but looking through the window in the door, it appeared that all of the students had already arrived. Pausing there, feeling apprehensive about going back to teaching, he was startled by a familiar voice next to him. "So, Doc, you goin' in, or aren't you?"

Jacob turned and saw his nemesis. "D'Angelo! Uh . . . I mean Michael. What are you doing here?"

"I'm here to observe."

"Observe? Observe what?"

"You. The Boss sent me to observe you on your first day as a member of Cosmos Industries Unlimited. You got hired."

Jacob returned to looking through the window at the classroom. "I'm honored, I guess."

"You should be. That's one tough employment exam."

Jacob laughed at his comment. "Yes, I agree with that." Jacob, still somewhat rattled over the morning's events, turned back to D'Angelo. "Who was in the car with you the other night when you were leaving the funeral home?"

"That was your grandfather Eli. I had picked him up. We had to get to Augusta National for an early tee time."

Jacob was stunned. "My grandfather never played golf as far as I know."

"Oh really? The old codger took me for a hundred and eighty clams. We were bettin' ten bucks a hole. Anyway, when we got done playing, there was a huge celebration at the nineteenth hole. That reverend Eli must have been one popular dude. He and Sarah were reunited and they were havin' a wonderful time. The band was incredible, and Elvis serenaded them as they danced all night. I suspect that party's still goin' on. Oh . . . by the way . . ." D'Angelo smiled at Jacob. "Your mother said she's proud of you and looks forward to seeing you soon."

"Soon? How soon?"

D'Angelo laughed. "Don't worry Doc . . . she's in a totally different time zone. You'll be on this ole' rock for a long time. The Boss has big plans for you."

Jacob was puzzled. "So, D'Angelo . . . Michael, are you the 'Grim Reaper' or something?"

"Nah! I like to think of myself as the 'Uber driver to Paradise'." Jacob chuckled and then turned back to looking in the classroom window. After standing motionless for a few moments, D'Angelo asked, "So . . . are you afraid of goin' in?"

"I'm not sure what to say to these people. So much has happened. I'm not the same person I was when I first began teaching this class."

"Well, you are now a member of Cosmos Industries Unlimited. Just open your mouth and the words will come right out. Trust me." D'Angelo moved toward the door. "I'm goin' in and gettin' my seat. You coming?"

"Yeah . . . sure. I'll be in there in a minute." Still stuck in the same place, another thought hit Jacob. "Hey . . . what if I need your help with something in the future? How do I find you?

THE WORDS OF A PROPHITT

    D'Angelo stopped and turned back to Jacob before getting to the door. "Just put on your ruby red slippers and click your heels three times."
    "I don't have any ruby red slippers."
    "Then hum 'In-A-Gadda-Da-Vida'. I love that song . . . killer drum solo."
    "Come on Michael . . . I'm being serious here."
    "Don't fret Doc . . . I've been coverin' the backsides of you Prophitt guys for ages . . . I'm never far away."
    D'Angelo reached for the door to enter the room. Jacob interrupted his entrance again with another question. "You aren't going to snore and disrupt the class again like you did last time, are you?"
    D'Angelo turned back laughing. "No way Doc! I'm all rested up. You won't even know I'm there."
    Jacob smiled. "Yeah . . . I bet!" D'Angelo grinned back at Jacob and entered the lecture hall. Hesitating for another moment, Jacob finally entered the classroom and was met with a standing ovation, which embarrassed him. He made his way over to the desk at the front of the room and sat on the corner of it, waiting for everyone to take their seats. Once it was quiet, Jacob replied, "Thank you. That was very humbling. I'm not sure if that was because you like me, or if you're just happy to be rid of Rabbi Weiss." That comment brought laughter from everyone in the room. Once the laughter subsided, Jacob continued, "It's good to be back. I have experienced a lot of changes in my life, as you might be able to ascertain from my appearance." That brought laughter from the class a second time. "I've missed not being here with all of you, learning together. Excuse me while I take a seat."
    Jacob moved around to the office chair behind the desk and slowly sat facing the students. He then continued,

"There is a term used in golf called a Mulligan. For those of you who aren't familiar with that term, I will try to explain. During a golf game, if you hit a terrible shot and there is no way to play it, you can ask for, or be offered a Mulligan, or in simple terms, a do-over. I come before all of you today asking for a Mulligan . . . a do-over. The reason I am making this request is because when I first walked into this classroom as your professor, I really didn't know why I was here. I thought my book was a farce, I was mad at the world, and I was questioning my faith in God. That wasn't fair to all of you. You have all chosen to teach the 'Word of God' because of your faith in Him, and here I was, a non-believer teaching you. I made a terrible golf shot. Now . . . all of that has changed."

Jacob was interrupted by a loud snore. He looked up at the last row of chairs expecting to see D'Angelo sleeping, only to see an empty chair. Smiling to himself, Jacob got up from his chair and moved back to sitting on the front of the desk where he had sat before so he could see the students better.

"Over the past few weeks, I have endured a crazy odyssey and have encountered many miraculous things. I don't want this to sound cliché, but I have literally been to the 'mountain' and met Satan himself, face-to-face, been in the presence of God, and heard God's voice. Since then, some other things have happened. First, my dysfunctional family has come together and we actually like each other. Admittedly, that probably doesn't count as a miracle from God. That is probably more in the common-sense category. But, this morning, my wife and I learned that our son, who had been diagnosed with an incurable disease, is healed. He is totally disease-free at this time!" Jacob paused and looked around the room at his students. Each and every one of them were leaning forward in their chairs, glued to every word Jacob spoke. "That, my friends, can only be attributed to the hands of God. So, I came before you as a non-believer . . . I stand before you now knowing that God definitely exists, and that He does answer prayers. I also learned that for your prayers to be answered, you must first be honest with yourself about what you are asking for. So, going back to the first day of class, I said that we were here to learn about the prophets and only the prophets, and that I did not want to get into any discussions about theology and faith in God. Well, that is all out the window! The truth is . . . this class is all about faith and God."

Suddenly, Jacob felt a presence, like someone was staring at him. He searched around the room and then finally glanced over at the door. Looking through the window directly at Jacob was the ghostly image of Jedediah Woodlock. Jedediah reached up and tipped his three-corner hat to Jacob. Jacob, now practically unphased by anything, nodded his acknowledgement. Jedediah winked at Jacob and then turned and walked out of view. Jacob smiled to himself, paused for a moment, and then got up from his desk and moved over to the podium. "Okay, we all have a lot of work to do, both here in this classroom and out in the world. Let's get started . . .

ANGELS IN DISGUISE

There are angels on the earth for sure
But how are we to know
We're skeptical of everything
Our lives do surely show

They seemingly are everywhere
The Bible says it's true
Put here by God Himself
To help with what we do

We have our family and our friends
We love them oh so much
They help us in our time of need
And often are our crutch

But if we searched a little more
And took our heed from God
Our lives would be much easier
Our road, not hard to trod

So, when a stranger speaks to you
Take heed in what they say
It could be an angel in disguise
To help along your way

Copyright © Sandra Romer-Alexander
November 3rd, 2000

www.ingramcontent.com/pod-product-compliance
Lightning Source LLC
Chambersburg PA
CBHW051356290426
44108CB00015B/2040